MONROE COLLEGE LIBRARY

3 7340 010870

D0221854

GENDER AND EVERYDAY LIFE

Why are we so insistent that women and men are different? This introduction to gender provides a fascinating and genuinely readable exploration of how society divides people into feminine women and masculine men. It explores gender as a way of seeing women and men as not just biological organisms, but as people shaped by their everyday social world. Examining how gender has been understood and lived in the past, and how it is understood and done differently by different cultures and groups within cultures, Mary Holmes considers the strengths and limitations of different ways of thinking and learning to 'do' gender.

Key sociological and feminist ideas about gender are covered, from Christine Pisan to Mary Wollstonecraft, and from symbolic interactionism to second-wave feminism through to the work of Judith Butler. The book illustrates gender with a range of familiar and contemporary examples: everything from nineteenth-century fashions in China and Britain, to discussions of what Barbie can tell us about gender in America, to the lives of working women in Japan. This book will be of great use and interest to students of gender studies, sociology and feminist theory.

Mary Holmes is Senior Lecturer in the Department of Sociology at Flinders University, Australia. She is currently co-writing a book (with Chris Beasley and Heather Brook) called *Adventures in Heterosexuality*, and is the author of *What is Gender?* She is coeditor of *Critical Concepts: The Sociology of the Body* (also published by Routledge).

DISCARDED

MONROE COLLEGE LIBRRARY
434 MAIN STREET
NEW ROCHELLE, NY 10801

THE NEW SOCIOLOGY

SERIES EDITOR: ANTHONY ELLIOTT, FLINDERS UNIVERSITY, AUSTRALIA

The New Sociology is a book series designed to introduce students to new issues and themes in social sciences today. What makes the series distinctive, as compared with other competing introductory textbooks, is a strong emphasis not just on key concepts and ideas but on how these play out in everyday life – on how theories and concepts are lived at the level of selfhood and cultural identities, how they are embedded in interpersonal relationships, and how they are shaped by, and shape, broader social processes.

Titles in the series:

Religion and Everyday Life
STEPHEN HUNT (2005)

Culture and Everyday Life
DAVID INGLIS (2005)

Community and Everyday Life
GRAHAM DAY (2005)

Consumption and Everyday Life
MARK W.D. PATERSON (2005)

Ethnicity and Everyday Life
CHRISTIAN KARNER (2007)

Globalization and Everyday Life
LARRY RAY (2007)

Risk, Vulnerability and Everyday Life
IAIN WILKINSON (2007)

Gender and Everyday Life
MARY HOLMES (2008)

Forthcoming titles in the series:

Self-Identity and Everyday Life
HARVIE FERGUSON (2008)

Cities and Everyday Life
DAVID PARKER (2008)

Nationalism and Everyday Life
JANE HINDLEY (2008)

The Body and Everyday Life
HELEN THOMAS (2008)

Media and Everyday Life
ELLIS CASHMORE (2009)

305.3
Hol

GENDER AND EVERYDAY LIFE

MARY HOLMES

Routledge
Taylor & Francis Group

LONDON AND NEW YORK

First published 2009
by Routledge
2 Park Square, Milton Park, Abingdon, Oxon, OX14 4RN

Simultaneously published in the USA and Canada
by Routledge
270 Madison Avenue, New York NY 10016

*Routledge is an imprint of the Taylor and Francis Group,
an informa business*

© 2009 Mary Holmes

Typeset in Garamond by
Swales & Willis Ltd, Exeter, Devon
Printed and bound in Great Britain
by TJ International Ltd, Padstow, Cornwall

All rights reserved. No part of this book may be reprinted or
reproduced or utilized in any form or by any electronic, mechanical
or other means, now known or hereafter invented, including
photocopying and recording, or in any information storage or
retrieval system, without permission in writing from the publishers.

British Library Cataloguing in Publication Data
A catalogue record for this book is available from the British Library

Library of Congress Cataloging in Publication Data
Gender and everyday life / Mary Holmes.
p. cm.— (The new sociology)
Includes bibliographical references and index.
ISBN 978–0–415–42348–9 (hbk)—ISBN 978–0–415–42349–6 (pbk)
—ISBN 978–0–203–92938–4 (ebk) 1. Sex role. 2. Sex
differences. 3. Gender identity. I. Title.
HQ1075.H63 2008
305.3—dc22
2008007770

ISBN10: 0–415–42348–1 (hbk)
ISBN10: 0–415–42349–X (pbk)
ISBN10: 0–203–92938–1 (ebk)

ISBN13: 978–0–415–42348–9 (hbk)
ISBN13: 978–0–415–42349–6 (pbk)
ISBN10: 978–203–92938–4 (ebk)

In memory of Mike Hepworth, fabulous mentor and all-round good bloke, and of my mother, Anita Holmes

CONTENTS

SERIES EDITOR'S FOREWORD

'The New Sociology' is a Series that takes its cue from massive social transformations currently sweeping the globe. Globalization, new information technologies, the techno-industrialization of warfare and terrorism, the privatization of public resources, the dominance of consumerist values: these developments involve major change to the ways people live their personal and social lives today. Moreover, such developments impact considerably on the tasks of sociology, and the social sciences more generally. Yet, for the most part, the ways in which global institutional transformations are influencing the subject-matter and focus of sociology have been discussed only in the more advanced, specialized literature of the discipline. I was prompted to develop this Series, therefore, in order to introduce students – as well as general readers who are seeking to come to terms with the practical circumstances of their daily lives – to the various ways in which sociology reflects the transformed conditions and axes of our globalizing world.

Perhaps the central claim of the Series is that sociology is fundamentally linked to the practical and moral concerns of everyday life. The authors in this Series – examining topics all the way from the body to globalization, from self-identity to consumption – seek to demonstrate the complex, contradictory ways in which sociology is a necessary and very practical aspect of our personal and public lives. From one angle, this may seem uncontroversial. After all, many classical sociological analysts as well as those associated with the classics of social theory emphasized the practical basis of human knowledge, notably Emile Durkheim, Karl Marx, Max Weber, Sigmund Freud and George Simmel, among many others. And yet there are major respects in which the professionalization of academic sociology during the latter period of the twentieth century led to a retreat from the everyday issues and moral basis of sociology itself. (For an excellent discussion of the changing relations between practical and professional sociologies see Charles Lemert, *Sociology After the Crisis*, second edition, Boulder: Paradigm, 2004.) As worrying as such a retreat from the practical and moral grounds of the discipline is, one of the main consequences of recent global transformations in the field of sociology has been a renewed emphasis on the mediation of everyday events and experiences by distant social forces, the intermeshing of the local and global in the production of social practices, and on ethics and moral responsibility at both the individual and collective levels. 'The New Sociology' Series traces out these concerns across the terrain of various themes and thematics, situating everyday social practices in the broader context of life in a globalizing world.

Without doubt, nowhere today do we see the impact of global institutional changes restructuring the terrain of everyday lived experience, as well as the intellectual preoccupations of disciplinary sociology, than in society's surging anxieties about gender. For some conservative critics, dramatic change in routine gender practice is the chief source of today's social ills; for others – including political progressives of various persuasions – gender lies at the core of current transformations of intimacy as well as alternative sexualities and lifestyles. In *Gender and Everyday Life*, Mary Holmes explores the peculiar place – troubled and troubling – of gender in contemporary society and culture. In this marvellously clear and compelling introduction to the key theoretical and political disputes over gender in sociology, Holmes develops a powerful overview of both classical and contemporary scholarship on gender categories.

Social theories of gender have been at the forefront of the most important debates in the social sciences and humanities over the last 25 years, and one of Mary Holmes' critical aims in this book is to unravel the wider cultural and social meanings attributed to gender – in both practical social life and professional sociology – over the years. In shining a light on the powers of gender in our everyday lives, Holmes deftly traces a number of social differences that structure, organize and solicit gendered and sexual identities. All these differences in body politics and social relations, socialized learning and cultural resistance, turn out to be fundamental to both our gendered lives and bodily investments – with every chapter offering a distinctive perspective on the paradoxes of gender. Gender, for Holmes, generates plenty of heat, framing how we move in and out of the identifications, pleasures and troubles of identities, structures of action and agency, and the management of sexual differences and bodily capabilities.

The liquid application of gender concepts, variously traced by Holmes through the sociological deployment of historical, comparative and critical perspectives, is responsible in our own time for many of the conflicts and tensions of sexed identities and their relation to forms of social exclusion. In this connection, Holmes' erudite analysis of gender sharpens our thinking, and indeed is itself good to think along with. If sex refers to biology and gender to sociology, what are the connections between the two? Is gender really just a supplement to anatomical sexual differences, or does it have a life of its own? Is gender autonomy possible, or are we forever subject and subordinate to sexual differences and gender norms? Does gender need to be updated, through a kind of theoretical 'extreme makeover', to better fit with the times and our lives in these times? How do gender belongings and exclusions interweave with social reproduction, power and hierarchy? What gender futures might we face? How significant is gender in shaping the direction of society and culture? Holmes proves an erudite guide to all these issues and more besides.

Gender, as Holmes makes clear, is central to social regulation in almost all societies. Gender is fundamental to our very existence, and for that reason societies solicit gendered rules and expectations around sexuality. In our own time of the early 2000s, these rules have been subject to considerable upheaval: from the so-called 'liberation of gender' through either commercial possibilities or postmodern sexual fluidities to the impact of queer theory and radical theorizing on gender categories. Certainly the growth of consumer culture, the acceleration of globalization and new patterns of work (principally short term and contract based) have tended to create transformed social conditions in which gender becomes a renewed political site for thinking about the pressures and compulsions of our lives today. In Holmes' synthetic vision of the variety of gender scenarios currently before us, and likely to come before us in the near future, the configuration of gender practice is up for grabs in novel and perhaps alarming ways. Holmes' *Gender and Everyday Life* is indeed a superb introduction to the sociological stakes of gender in our fast globalizing world.

Anthony Elliott
Adelaide, 2008

ACKNOWLEDGEMENTS

Two people who were very important to me died while I was writing this book. I lost my mother in September 2007, and earlier that year was shocked by the sudden death of my friend and former colleague Mike Hepworth. My mother always treated others with great care and kindness, but could be a sharp yet amusing critic if someone was spouting ignorant or prejudiced nonsense. If there were mother evaluation forms she would have scored top of the scale. Mike was the most constructive critic I have ever met. I was exceedingly fond of the way he would ask: 'But do you really think that?' Mike always made you think and think well. He also always made us all laugh, about everything – including sociology. Mike provided a model of how to be a sociologist, and indeed an academic, while being a kind, encouraging and gloriously funny human being. He was enormously influential in how I learnt and continue to do sociology.

Other thanks go to Anthony Elliot for asking me to write this book and for his general encouragement of my work. Again thanks to my former colleagues at the University of Aberdeen, who were especially important last year as we all struggled with the loss of Mike. Particular thanks to David Inglis for giving me guidance based on writing his own excellent book for this series, *Culture and*

Everyday Life. I also want to thank Karen O'Reilly; we did a good double act in our teaching at Aberdeen and I am sure that some of her ideas have ended up in my work, as no doubt have some of David's. I just hope some of mine may have ended up in theirs. I also want to thank all my colleagues at Flinders. In Adelaide there are people who provide extra special intellectual and emotional sustenance and sometimes actual food as well (and I like food). In no particular order: Anna Mallyon, Riaz Hassan, Chris Beasley, Heather Brook, Daniel Chaffee and Brent Everitt. Also thank you to Jane Haggis for being truly collegiate and to Carolyn Corkindale, for whom the title 'Research Assistant' seems inadequate to describe her intelligence, skills and helpfulness. May this book, with all its flaws, be acceptable as a small memoriam to Mike and Mum, and as a testament of how lucky I am to have worked with all these people.

INTRODUCTION: GENDER AND EVERYDAY LIFE

Think about what you have done so far today. How much of it would be different and how much the same if you were a member of the opposite sex? It is not just a matter of having different bits to wash in the shower. Did you shave your face or not? Did you apply make-up? How did you adorn your body once cleaned? Were jewellery, frills and high heels involved? When you ate breakfast did you count every calorie or worry about your lack of muscle? Did you eat breakfast at all? When you left the house how did your day differ from that of your siblings or friends of the opposite sex? Did you go to different types of jobs, attend lectures in different subjects, play different types of sport, have different conversations, different worries, engage in or imagine different types of careers? Maybe you did, but maybe there were a lot of similarities. Contrary to the way we talk a lot of the time, women and men are not different species. Yet everyday life is organized in ways that constantly distinguish women from men.

People tend to believe that women and men are naturally different, that they have different bodies, different biology, different psychology and therefore they act differently. The problem with this argument is that it usually suggests that how women and men live their everyday lives cannot or even should not be changed. But as most young people will tell you, the world is not the same as it was for their parents or grandparents, and they should not be expected to behave in the same way. What sociology can do is help us understand to what extent there are differences between women and men, why, and how significant they are. It can also help us understand change. It does this by looking at the way in which the social environment shapes women's and men's lives differently, how it genders them.

GENDERED LANGUAGE AND GENDERING EVERYDAY LIFE

In examining gender, sociologists and others in similar disciplines have developed a shorthand for discussing sometimes complex ideas. In other words, there is some special language used in the sociology of gender. Key terms (in bold type) are explained as they arise within each chapter, but there are some oft-used concepts that are worth mentioning here in order to introduce sociological thinking on gender in everyday life.

One of the most important things that sociologists do is distinguish between sex and gender. **Sex** refers to whether a person is considered female or male, based on the kind of body they have. **Gender** describes the ideas and practices that constitute femininity and masculinity. As we will see, male and female and masculine and feminine are not necessarily clear and opposite categories. Some people may have bodies and/or act in ways that do not neatly fit the labels male/masculine or female/feminine. And whether sex really describes something different from gender is open to question. However, it is important as a starting point to think of sex as about the bodily bits we have and gender as about social meanings.

Sociologists are interested in the **social construction** of gender, which means looking at how the way that society is organized shapes us into particular kinds of women and men. This shaping happens through large-scale social organization and through everyday interactions that we usually take for granted. For example, on the large scale, social institutions such as family, school, the workplace and the media teach us that girls should act in certain ways, such as being caring, and boys in different ways, such as being strong and independent. This process of teaching us how to behave is called **socialization** and it is highly gendered. But these institutions not only pass on ideas about how girls and boys are expected to act but channel girls and boys into doing different kinds of things. Girls and boys are dressed in different kinds of clothes, do different school subjects, usually end up in different jobs and are portrayed differently in everything from magazines to movies to television shows. From birth, girl children and boy children are treated differently, and every day of our lives involves interacting with other people according to their gender. We talk to girls/women differently about different things, assuming they are more delicate and will be interested in, say, clothes or children or cooking. Meanwhile, boys/men are treated as though they are tough and likely to be interested in sport or cars. Differences can be a good thing, however it is often women who have been thought different from men, who are assumed to be 'normal' and superior to women. Sociologists challenge such common-sense ideas.

While many people now believe that women and men are equal, this book will show that societies are still organized in ways that tend to benefit men more than they benefit women. We live within a **patriarchy**, a society largely controlled by men and in which men usually have a greater share of the rewards (both in terms of wealth and status) available. Even if men are uncomfortable with this and would like to change it, they still benefit from living within a male-dominated society. Sociologists have noted that gender is a major boundary around which resources and prestige and power are divided, with the majority of women often struggling to keep control over their lives. Therefore, in understanding gender it is important to examine and explain the apparent **inequalities** between men and women, and how they impact on people in everyday life.

The important thing about sociological views of gender is that change is thought possible. The problem with many arguments which insist that women and men are 'naturally' different is that it is assumed that things therefore will or should always stay as they are. Although inequalities are persistent they are not inevitable and sociology allows us to imagine that we could organize our world in a way that would benefit women and men more equally.

The everydayness of gender is central to this book. Life is lived mostly in the detail and much of that detail is taken for granted. Women put on make-up in the morning without really thinking about why. Men shave or trim their beards, but seldom stop to ponder these practices. In unusual circumstances, or if things go 'wrong', people are sometimes jogged into reflecting on the constant distinctions made between women and men. For example, in a busy cinema women may wonder why they are queuing for the women's toilets while the men waltz quickly in and out of the men's. This is a fairly trivial example of things going 'wrong' but small disruptions can be enough to upset the taken-for-grantedness. This small inconvenience raises several questions: Why do we have public toilets designated as either men's or women's when at home everyone shares the same toilet? Why are there not queues forming at the men's toilets? Possible answers are that Western culture views the expelling of human waste as shameful and disgusting, and so there is thought to be a need to protect women and men who are strangers from witnessing each other's bodily functions so that sexual mystique can be maintained. Also, common differences in women's and men's bodies, the kinds of clothing they wear and the types of toilets provided (men can use urinals) make it quicker for men to go to the toilet than women. This means that more cubicles are needed in women's toilets but that has not often been taken into account by planners, architects and developers, who are conscious mostly of costs (Edwards and McKie 1996). It is how the social environment is organized that leaves women waiting for the loo. The 'trick' of sociology is to turn a fresh eye on such social organization, including everyday gender practices. One famous formulation of how this 'trick' works is called the sociological imagination.

THE SOCIOLOGICAL IMAGINATION AND GENDER

The sociological imagination is a way of understanding the world that sees individuals as a product of the social world in which they live. The phrase comes from a book of that name by the American sociologist C. Wright Mills (1959). Mills argues that what sociologists, and indeed everyone, can do to better understand the world is to consider how each person's life is caught up in the history of their times. It is easy to illustrate what this means in relation to differences between women's and men's lives. Imagine you were a young, lower-middle-class Englishwoman in the late nineteenth century. You might write about your day in a diary:

10 February 1898

I really have had no time to come here before, and as usual, now I am here I have forgotten all my deeds. On Sunday Ewart and his sister Nellie came to ask us to tea in the afternoon. It was a very long way to his house which is 108 Heigham Road, East Ham. There are six of them alive and six dead. Mrs Johnson is very nice.

On Monday afternoon I went up to the day school to tell Mrs Osborne that Daisy and I had left. I have not been for weeks. I have been to the Doctor's four times and he says I am not strong enough for teaching and so I am going to stay at home and help Mother for a little while with the blouse work she sometimes does for a friend. Daisy is going as an apprentice to a dressmaker next week I think. Mrs Osborne was sorry and said all the nice girls were leaving. Also that she would be pleased to see us any afternoon we had to spare. In the evening we went to night school.

(Ruth, cited in Thompson 1987: 20–21)

This is a real diary entry by a 13-year-old called Ruth. It would contrast with that of a young man at the same time, as well as being different from the everyday life of a young woman today. She writes in a diary, not an online blog, she sends letters rather than texts to her best friend. She walks a long way to a friend's house rather than being driven. Ruth notes rather casually that only six of her friend's twelve brothers and sisters are still living; but it was common then for children to die before they were five. Ruth is leaving school at the age of 13 and about to start work, helping her mother sew blouses at home. Even had she been able to afford more education, universities had only just become open to women, and only the most privileged women went. She could not look forward to voting when she turned 18 as women were not given the right to vote in Britain until 1918, and then they had to be 30. However, as a result of new laws passed in the 1890s, if Ruth married she would be able to continue to legally own property after marriage, unlike her mother whose property automatically became her husband's. Meanwhile, if Ruth had a brother he may have found his job as a secretary or clerk was disappearing as the invention of the typewriter and the increased numbers of women who could be paid less in the workforce saw clerical work change from a male to a largely female occupation (Rendall 1985; Lowe 1987). Indeed it is clerical work that Ruth ends up doing. Changes in society, in social and historical conditions, have consequences for the kinds of lives that individual women and men can lead.

History, as Mills uses it, does not just mean what happened in the past, but refers to the wider circumstances within which people live. Giddens' (1986: 13) interpretation of Mills is useful in understanding these circumstances. He says that they can be comprehended by looking at the past, by comparing how different groups of people do things, and by thinking critically. This version of the sociological imagination as historical, comparative and critical, forms the central framework for this book so I want to spend a little time examining each of the aspects noted, and how they help us understand gender and everyday life.

HISTORY, GENDER AND EVERYDAY LIFE

Small people get caught up in large events. What it means for someone to be a woman or a man is different depending on the historical period in which they live. Drawing loosely on nineteenth-century research by Friederich Engels (1969/1845) and later investigations by scholars such as Sheila Rowbotham (1972), I want to think more about an individual's day and how each part of that day will differ depending on the time and place in which they live. What time someone gets up will depend on what kind of work they have to perform that day. Prior to the Industrial Revolution people usually worked on the land or in cottage industries and so they didn't travel to work. Before the mid-twentieth century only a small proportion of mothers went out to paid work, so the time they got up was related to their children's ages and timetables, as well as how much work they did in getting husbands off to their jobs. The kinds of things that people did in the morning differed. Before indoor plumbing was available, washing oneself was likely to be cursory or non-existent. The kind of clothes that women and men put on were very different to those worn today; prior to the 1920s women did not wear trousers, for instance. Before most of our food was mass produced, preparing breakfast involved rather more effort than pouring out a bowl of cornflakes, and many women may have had to go out to milk the cow to get the milk for the porridge or to rise especially early to light the fire in the range and perhaps start baking some bread. When most of the population still worked in agriculture men of the peasant classes would no doubt be up at dawn and do a few hours of backbreaking work in the fields before returning to eat breakfast. Women of the same class were also likely to be out working on the land, but were also expected to prepare food for the men's return. Schooling was not made compulsory in much of Europe, the British Empire and America until the 1870s, and until then children of the working classes were likely to be at work, doing dangerous jobs in the new factories, or down the mines or cleaning chimneys in the houses of the wealthy. The older girls in a family were likely to be looking after their younger brothers and sisters while their parents worked. It was difficult for nineteenth-century women to control their fertility, and the paid and unpaid work they did was increased by the relentless arrival of new additions to the family – although many children died in their first five years. Indeed, many women died in childbirth; therefore death was much more a feature of everyday life than it is in the present day. In many communities it was the women who prepared the bodies of the deceased to be laid out and did much of the work of providing for mourners. Whatever work a day had involved, the hours were long. Men might enjoy a drink at the end of a hard day, perhaps at the local pub. However, even in the mid-twentieth century in Britain and its former colonies, women were prohibited from entering most 'public' bars, and 'respectable' women would have entered lounge bars only in the company of male relatives. When it finally came time to retire to bed most Victorian children would have shared a bed with other siblings and slept in the same room as their parents. Clearly what women and men got up to after dark would have been rather constrained by such circumstances. All or some of these things may be unfamiliar to those of you reading this now, because of changes in the wider world in which we live.

A jumble of things are described above, but sociologists can make sense of the kinds of changes mentioned by looking at the patterns of large-scale social changes. Mills (1959) talks about this in terms of drawing a distinction between private troubles and public issues. If one woman was thrown out of a pub for drinking too much that might be a private trouble; however, if any woman who set foot in a public bar was breaking the law, that was a public issue. If one young man failed to find work in times of prosperity because he was thought unreliable that was a private trouble; it became a public issue if many young men found it hard to get work because women and children were cheaper to employ within the new factories springing up in the eighteenth and nineteenth centuries. If a married woman chooses to give up her job because she wants to stay at home and care for her young children, that may be a personal decision; however, if getting married meant that you *had* to give up your job, as it did for married women teachers even in the early twentieth century, that was a public issue to do with social expectations and social organization around gender.

The major pattern that sociologists see in bringing social change, including that relating to gender, was the shift from an agricultural to an industrial society, which brought about modernity. **Modernity** is a phase in which everyday life lost its connection to tradition and people had to develop new ways of living. Most of the population moved from rural to urban areas during the nineteenth century and these urban areas rapidly grew. Instead of relying on farming and small craft industries to meet their daily needs most people had to work for wages, often in appalling conditions within factories. Having worked at, around or very close to home, now many people went 'out' to work and this separation of home and work had a profound impact on family life, especially as child labour became less acceptable and pressure was put on women to stay at home and care for children, even though working families could not survive on the male wage alone. Individual women and men faced new possibilities, but also new problems as a result of the huge changes happening around them. These changes continue and sociologists, as we shall see, are currently debating how to talk about them. Some argue that we are now in late modernity, where processes of individualization (people being encouraged and/or forced to rely on themselves) and globalization (the speeded-up connections between parts of the world) are crucial in shaping the everyday lives of women and men. But not all women and men are affected in the same ways.

COMPARATIVE APPROACHES TO GENDER

The point of comparisons is to establish that gender is shaped differently by different social environments. This assists in understanding that differences between women and men are not simply a product of their biology. If biology determined women's and men's behaviour, we would expect all women and all men to be more or less the same. However, this is not the case. So far I have made a lot of generalizations, and sociology can help us talk about what was and is happening to *most* people, but it also helps us see how different groups are affected differently by what is going on in society. One of the major differences in which sociologists have been interested since the discipline emerged almost 200 years ago, is class. Differences between cultures and other ways of grouping people to make comparisons are also discussed.

Class describes a grouping of people who share a similar degree of wealth and status within a society. Karl Marx, considered one of the founders of sociology, concentrated on class as being about the kind of work people did. He distinguished the main classes in modernity as the capitalists, or bourgeoisie, who owned the factories and other businesses, and the workers, or proletariat, who had to sell their labour to survive. He thought that classes were inevitably in conflict with each other and that was how social change happened. Max Weber, another founder of sociology, thought that it was not only the work people did and how much money they had that was important, but the amount of prestige they had. For example, some aristocrats may have no money left but are still highly regarded; meanwhile some prostitutes may make a lot of money but are not respected. Class is a complex issue, and class divisions shift, but it is still a useful category. It helps us understand how and why different groups share unequally in the resources and rewards society has to offer. What is crucial in terms of this book is that not all women are the same and not all men are the same. Working-class women are likely to share similar experiences of gender that are different to those of middle-class women.

Patterns can be seen connecting upper-class men's lives, for whom economic privilege and status will give them advantages not shared by working-class men. Some examples are given in Chapter 2 about how ways of being feminine differ in different classes, thus illustrating social variations in gender.

The examination of **cultural differences** in gender is another way in which the importance of the social can be established. This is the point at which sociology overlaps with, or turns to, anthropology. Anthropologists have tended to study traditional, non-Western societies, while sociologists have looked at modern Western societies. This is not a hard-and-fast distinction, but whether comparing Papua New Guinea and the United States, or Scotland and Australia, the differences between cultures reveal a great deal about how gender is socially constructed. One society may have completely different ways of understanding and doing femininity and masculinity to another. For example, in Chapter 1, we will discuss tribes who have other categories to classify people in between 'feminine' and 'masculine'. Yet these are not the only differences to note.

Other comparisons can be made between women and men of different ages, with different locations in relation to power, or at different stages of life – for example, before and after having families. Of course, not all women and men form the same kinds of families or relationships, as Chapter 3 notes. There we use quite a common comparison within sociology, that between groups doing things in conventional ways and those who are different or 'deviant'. Sometimes the non-conventional groups are at the fore-front of social change and this may be the case with those with new ways of organizing their intimate lives that move away from traditional ideas about gender. Alternatively, it can be useful to compare more powerful groups with less powerful groups. One example of this appears in Chapter 4, where, having looked at histories of women's resistance, we look at the rather different project of men who resist norms around masculinity. Compar-isons can primarily be descriptive, outlining how one group of people differs from another. However, they can also be a crucial background to and/or component in critical thinking.

CRITICAL THINKING

Sociologies of gender are not simply about differences between women and men but about the social hierarchies and inequalities that arise from the social construction of gender. A critical stance on gender involves thinking about why men usually have more privileges and power than women. Sociology strives to go beyond describing the social world and endeavours to understand why it is as it is and how it could be otherwise. Critical thinking is to do with examining the strengths and limitations of various ideas and ways of life. In many ways a critical approach within sociology includes the elements already discussed. A critical approach to gender is assisted by looking at how gender has had other meanings and been done very differently at different times and within different cultures, different classes and other different social groups. Sociologists of gender try to weigh up the advantages and disadvantages of these different ways of doing gender. Generally, past ways of doing things may have been more restrictive for women; however, there may have been some ways in which women had more control over their lives – for example, there are disadvantages to current expectations that women *both* have careers and be highly involved as mothers. Similarly, care needs to be taken in assuming that men have more control over women in other cultures. This usually underestimates the limitations many Western women face in their lives, and lumps together all non-Western men and women as somehow 'backward'. There are many examples that might challenge these stereotypes – one is to consider women in political power. The African nation of Rwanda currently has the highest percentage of women in a national parliament; almost half the MPs are women, whereas in the United States only 16 per cent of those in the House of Representatives are women (Inter-parliamentary Union 2007).

Another crucial aspect of thinking critically is to examine existing debates around sociological issues such as gender. Not all sociologists agree, and the task of sociological thinking is not to establish the truth but to try to forge better understandings of how the world works. Various explanations, or theories, are forwarded by different groups of sociologists and other scholars in trying to understand gender. In the critical section of each chapter, I evaluate some of these different sets of ideas, and give an assessment of some of their strengths and limitations. I encourage you as readers to add your own critical assessment to mine. And, in order to stimulate critical thinking further, I offer a whole chapter on the future of gender, the main purpose of which is to examine ways in which gender may be done very differently in years to come.

HOW THE BOOK IS ORGANIZED

To begin to imagine different possibilities requires understanding how society presently divides people according to whether they are women or men, expecting them to think, act and feel differently. Gender will be explored as the socially constructed and socially practised differences between masculinity and femininity. This means looking at how people live their everyday lives in a world where what it means to be a woman or a man is uncertain and changing. The framework of the book will be based on the interpretation of the sociological imagination I have outlined as involving historical, comparative and critical analysis (Mills 1959; Giddens 1986: 13). To understand gender will involve seeing how femininity and masculinity have been understood and lived in the past (history), how they are understood and done differently by different cultures and groups within cultures (comparative), and what might be the strengths and limitations of different ways of thinking and doing gender (critical analysis). This understanding will be clearer if we constantly keep in mind how gender is lived in everyday life. Therefore the book considers gender as something that is lived and experienced from within particular types of bodies. First, we look at the problems in seeing bodies as sexed bodies that make us behave in 'feminine' or 'masculine' ways. Then we explore the emergence of sociological arguments that gender is not something we naturally *are*, but something we learn to *do*. It is something that is done within socially organized relations to other people, relationships that involve power and inequalities. Gender is also not something that we just passively take on board, and Chapter 4 considers some of the many ways in which people might resist gender conventions and do things differently. The book closes by considering what the future of gender might be, given scientific and social developments that increasingly alter bodies and blur boundaries between 'women' and 'men'.

1

SEXED BODIES?

People have different-sized ears. Imagine that society was organized around a distinction between people with big ears and those with small ears. Whenever we filled out a form, instead of ticking either the 'female' or the 'male' boxes we would have to tick the 'big ears' or the 'small ears' box. Toilets would have different pictures on them; rather than 🛉 and 🛉 they might be something like this:

There might be jobs that are thought more suitable for people with big ears. People might say that big ears make good counsellors, they are so good at listening. There might be different clothing associated with each group. Perhaps big ears never wear hats, whereas small ears sometimes do. And perhaps small ears in some countries are not entitled to vote, because it is thought that they cannot hear political arguments properly and therefore cannot make reasonable decisions. But surely this is a ridiculous example? What about people with medium-sized ears, what would happen to them? Well, much the same as happens to those people who are neither female nor male.

Not all bodies can be categorized as either female or male. There are more than two variations of sex that naturally occur. Genetically women and men are overwhelmingly similar. Each person has around three billion base pairs of genes, which form 46 chromosomes (23 pairs), of which only one pair determines sex. If this is XX the person will be female; if it is XY, they will be male. However, other combinations regularly occur. There are people who are XXY, some who are XXYY, and many others. These combinations sometimes produce individuals who are intersex, in so far as they do not comfortably fit the categories 'male' or 'female'. For example, Turner's syndrome is where a child is born with one X chromosome on the pair determining sex, and the other missing. Although Turner's syndrome children have female genitalia, their ovaries do not function and they may need hormones to help them develop secondary female sex characteristics, such as breasts, at puberty. Similarly, another syndrome, called Klinefelter, arises when, as well as an XY pair, a child has an extra 47th chromosome, which is an X. This leads typically to small testes and at puberty these individuals may have little body hair, some breast development and do not produce sperm (Fausto-Sterling 2000, 2002). Broadly speaking those with Turner's syndrome might still be 'women' and those with Klinefelter might be 'men' (Sax 2002), but they nevertheless disturb our usual definitions of what makes someone female or male. Even more challenging to those categories are the babies occasionally born with what could be either a small penis or a large clitoris. Their chromosomal sex may not clearly fit the pattern of XX = woman and XY = man. It is difficult to determine the sex of these and the other children sometimes born with sexual characteristics that are some combination of male and female (e.g. with some form of penis as well as a vagina).

These people have usually been called hermaphrodites. If you use broad definitions of 'intersex', including, for example, persons with Turner's and Klinefelter syndromes, it is estimated that around 17 people in every 1,000 fall into a category somewhere between male and female (Fausto-Sterling 2002; Hird 2004).

Although *most* people are either female or male, the mere existence of people who cannot easily be classified as one or the other raises all sorts of questions about how our everyday lives are organized around making a clear distinction between 'men' and 'women'. Intersex people present a problem in terms of how society operates (Kessler and McKenna 1985/1978). How will they know whether to tick the F or the M box on forms, which public toilets to use, whether or not to wear a skirt, to what welfare benefits they are entitled, which sports events to enter? How will other people know whether to call them 'Ms' or 'Mr', or how to interact with them? So problematic is being intersex considered that babies with the condition are almost always submitted to medically unnecessary surgery to *make* them fit either the female or the male category (Hird 2004; see also Intersex Society of North America 2006). They are then expected to develop an identity to match. But even people who are born as definitely female or definitely male do not always develop an identity to match. Some women are described as 'masculine', some men act in 'feminine' ways. However, it is usually implied that what is 'normal' and 'natural' is for females to act in feminine ways and males to act in masculine ways.

People often talk about women as being *naturally* smaller, weaker, more emotional, rather irrational, more caring, and so on. Men are thought to be larger, more prone to aggression, less emotional, rational and perhaps more selfish. When they say this, people seem to mean that the way men's and women's bodies differ makes them behave differently. But do we overemphasize differences and underemphasize similarities?

In everyday life the differences between women's bodies and men's bodies are constantly reinforced. Once a baby is born and its sex made clear (usually by a quick look at its genitals), it is declared that 'it's a girl' or 'it's a boy'. **Sex** is the bodily based classification of people into female or male. Once the child's sex is established (by surgical means if necessary) then all sorts of social expectations begin to operate about what the child will be like, how he/she will act and how other people should treat him or her. Sociologists do not think that sex determines people's behaviour. For instance, they challenge common-sense interpretations of science which assume that testosterone causes men to be aggressive. As we will see this does not mean that sociologists think bodies are unimportant. Rather they think that how we use and understand bodies depends on the particular society and time in which we live. To help think about the way in which our social environment creates particular ways of thinking about and being feminine and masculine, sociologists use the term **gender**. It can be helpful to define sex as referring to the physical and chromosomal features that (usually) produce a female or a male human being. Gender describes the social expectations, rules and norms attached to femininity and masculinity. Sex corresponds to male and female; gender to feminine and masculine.

The sociology of gender is about the way in which social factors shape how women and men act. The term gender was not introduced until the 1970s. Prior to that sociologists talked about 'sex roles' (Parsons and Bales 1956) and 'the management of sex' (Garfinkel 1967). As a concept, gender was helpful in challenging common-sense ideas about sex as a 'natural' and unchangeable fact arising from anatomy. Gender could help make arguments about men and women as socially constructed, and inequalities as therefore 'man-made' and open to change. However, it is now thought that too sharp a distinction between sex as biological and gender as social has limitations, and that bodies need to be part of understanding gender. The way in which we understand and organize everyday life around differences between women and men both draws on particular understandings about sexed (male and female) bodies and produces gendered (masculine and feminine) bodies.

As I explained in the Introduction, I want to use an adapted version of the sociological imagination to explain how sex/gender works in people's everyday lives. To understand how bodies are shaped by ideas and by what 'women' and 'men' do, we can look at how understandings of sex have changed across history. The 'facts' are not always clear, and present interpretations of what constitutes femaleness and maleness might change. Also we can compare the varying ways different cultures have of understanding sexed bodies and their relationship to gendered ways of acting. The final and crucial part of using the sociological imagination to understand sexed bodies in relation to everyday life, is thinking critically. This means thinking about the strengths and limitations of current ideas and practices around bodies in relation to sex and gender.

A HISTORY OF SEX

One way of appreciating that sexed bodies do not entirely determine how women and men act in everyday life is to look at past scientific 'facts' about the body. We can see that our understanding of how bodies work has changed. For example, in the nineteenth century many scientists thought that higher education would make women exhausted and infertile. Their reproductive systems, it was argued, required considerable energy, which should not be 'wasted' on book learning, and they should therefore not be admitted to universities (Delamont 1978). These ideas were related to theories at the time which thought that women's reproductive capacities made them irrational. The notion of hysteria as a female 'disease' had long existed, the name being taken from the Greek for womb (*hystera*), but interest in the 'disease' peaked during the Victorian era – just as women were demanding a role beyond home and family. The condition was thought to arise from a 'wandering womb'. It was argued that this shifting of the womb happened in women who delayed childbearing. The symptoms of the disease were many, so that virtually anything could be labelled as hysterical. In particular, any behaviour thought wild or irrational, any angriness, screaming, crying or fainting, could be thought abnormal and women thought in need of curing. Treatment varied from psychoanalysis to radical surgical intervention (Turner 1984; Bordo 1989; Foucault 1990). The case of 'Annemarie', in Victorian New Zealand, is an extreme example of the treatment that could be given to nineteenth-century Western women labelled 'hysterical':

> On boxing day in 1886, when Annemarie was aged seventeen, she went on to a picnic and then to a ball in Invercargill. Around midnight she apparently began raving about love and religion and had to be brought home. Her mother reported that these events happened at her menstrual period. Cold baths followed by friction were tried to calm Annemarie from her bouts of singing, praying, laughing and crying. After a few months she 'lapsed into profound melancholy' and was eventually sent to Ashburn hall, a private asylum in Dunedin. . . . Annemarie's family consulted their local doctor about her condition; he suggested that some improvement might follow if she were completely unsexed by the removal of her ovaries and clitoris. . . . On 20 July [1890], Dr Ferdinand Batchelor, one of Dunedin's leading medical luminaries, assisted by three other doctors including Truby King, removed Annemarie's fallopian tubes, ovaries and clitoris. . . . Nearly a month after the operation Annemarie exhibited no mental change.
>
> (Brookes 1991: 15–16)

It is easy to laugh and/or be outraged at these outdated ideas and their consequences, but the point of discussing them is to recognize that science is always a 'best guess' based on the evidence available. It is interesting to speculate which of the ideas presently accepted as scientific 'fact' will be laughable or thought 'barbaric' in the future. The point is that scientific theories change, and that those changes can be looked at from a sociological point of view. From this point of view we can see that scientists live and work within particular times and cultures, and what they are interested in and how they interpret what they find are influenced by their social surroundings and the ideas of the time (cf. Laqueur 1990). This applies to the scientific investigation of sex.

Prior to the eighteenth century, Western scientists tended to think about male and female as different expressions of the one human body. As the historian Thomas Laqueur (1990) argues, in this 'one-sex' model female genitalia were described as a less-developed version of fully unfolded and 'perfected' male genitals. The ovaries were thought equivalent to the testes, the shaft of the vagina and the clitoris were seen as a (mostly) interior version of the penis. This representation of sexual difference corresponded to widespread ideas about femininity and masculinity as attributes of all individuals. It is likely that Judeo-Christian myths were influential because in the pre-modern world most people got their information about the world from the Church. The idea of sex as a variation, rather than an absolute distinction, fits well with the familiar story of Eve as created from Adam's rib. In medieval times both women and men were thought to have 'feminine' aspects to their character; and masculinity was frequently associated with things women sometimes did, without them being thought mannish. Feminine and masculine described types of behaviour not types of people (Laqueur 1990). Indeed this idea has not completely disappeared, but ways of seeing sex started to gradually shift in the 1700s, and from 1800 a two-sex model began to gain dominance.

The two-sex model of sex emphasizes male and female bodies as utterly different and indeed opposite. Differences in male and female genitalia start to be seen as crucial (Laqueur 1990). In addition, everything from body shape (Jordanova 1989) to hormones (Oudshoorn 1994) began to be seen in terms of a 'normal' male form to which a 'deviant' female form was opposed. One interesting example of this shift is how skeletons were represented. Before the mid-eighteenth century scientific drawings of skeletons tended just to be labelled 'human'. However, from late that century separate drawings began to be made of female skeletons, which emphasized differences rather than the underlying similarities. One of the most widely adopted eighteenth-century drawings of the 'female' skeleton was by a woman anatomist. She drew the skull as quite small in proportion to the body. This was despite the fact that prevailing science had found women's skulls to be larger in proportion to their bodies than men's. However, this inaccurate drawing was adopted rather than others available, probably because it helped confirm ideas at the time that saw a large skull as a sign of intelligence. Even in more accurate portrayals the skeletons drawn were carefully selected to fit the ideal of a man or woman at the time, and sometimes skulls or other bones from a different body were used when the main skeleton did not quite live up to the ideal for its sex. The main difference portrayed in drawing female skeletons was the pelvis bones, which were drawn larger than male's. This emphasis came from new desires to show that women were best suited to having babies. All this happened around the time that concerns were emerging about population growth. Racist fears prompted much debate about the need for white women of the higher classes to concentrate on having and raising children in order to ensure the survival and continued dominance of 'the white race' (Schiebinger 1989). A woman's reproductive role began to be promoted as her proper duty, and early arguments (e.g. Wollstonecraft 1985/1792) about women's rights to entry to the public world of work and politics were partly a response to these efforts to restrict women's lives to the family sphere. 'Scientific' views about women's biology as essentially different (and inferior) to men's gained prominence from the 1750s, and had to be challenged by those wanting to argue against the exclusion of women from higher education, the professions and political decision making. Such understandings of the differences between women and men as founded in their supposedly different 'natural' bodies have continued to be prominent throughout the nineteenth and twentieth centuries and into the twenty-first.

The belief that bodies are clearly sexed, and that this explains behaviour, is still common, but it is important to remember that the emphasis on bodily difference is of fairly recent historical origin. This indicates that sex is not a matter of simple scientific fact, but a category that requires interpretation. What sex means and how bodies are understood to be 'sexed' changes over time. It also varies in different cultures, further illustrating that sex and gender are socially, not just biologically, constructed.

COMPARING DIFFERENT IDEAS ABOUT SEXED/GENDERED BODIES

Different cultures think about and go about being women and men in different ways in their everyday lives. Not all cultures think about sex or do gender in terms of male versus female and masculine versus feminine. How they think sex is related to gender and to sexuality is often also different. Here I will outline some of the alternative ways of thinking about bodies as sexed, gendered and sexual. These include sex/gender systems that have a 'third sex' and/or 'third gender' (Herdt 1994). Even where a culture shares the 'two-sex' model, it does not necessarily have the same expectations as Anglo-American peoples about what is 'womanly' and what is 'manly'. Everyday tasks assigned to women and men, and expectations about how they will act vary from one culture to another.

Third sex/gender

Within the First Nation peoples of North America, everyday life was traditionally organized to allow for a category of people who are not simply men/masculine or women/feminine. The generic name for these people is 'berdaches', but within particular tribes they will have particular names, such as *nádleheé* in the Navajo, or *Ihamana* among the Zuni. It seems that, most commonly, berdaches were biological males who in everyday life did many of the things usually associated with women. They might dress like women, undertake the crafts and other work usually done by women and usually engaged in sex with men once matured. However, there were female berdaches and, whether male or female, many wore clothing somewhere between the usual 'masculine' and 'feminine' forms of dress. Some berdaches performed both 'feminine' and 'masculine' tasks – for example, carrying out weaving (usually women's work) at the same time as being a medicine man (usually men's work), or being a squaw (performing a conventional women's role) but also gaining renown for hunting skills (hunting usually being done only by men). It is argued that male berdaches therefore constitute a third, and female berdaches a fourth, gender. They were usually revered as special individuals and, rather than being seen as somewhere between 'masculine' and 'feminine', there were separate sets of expectations among Native American peoples about how berdaches would act, and what kinds of tasks they would carry out in their society (Roscoe 1994).

The tasks people do in their everyday lives are important in identifying their gender, because not all cultures require the same kind of match with sexed bodies as in the West (cf. Kessler and McKenna 1985/1978). In India, there is a category of people who might be understood as 'feminine', although Western definitions might struggle to put them in a sex category. *Hijras* follow a goddess known as Bahuchara Mata. The belief is that if men are sexually impotent with women they are called upon to be castrated and to follow the goddess by dressing and acting like women. Through Western eyes *hijras* might be characterized as men without penises who follow feminine gender roles; but this might misunderstand how they are seen within Indian culture. Cultural beliefs about women and men are that they are essentially different and born to fulfil complementary roles. The feminine role is viewed as potentially destructive because it is believed women are sexually insatiable, but femininity is also recognized as a creative power. *Hijras* therefore have a religious and social role serving the goddess, and performing at weddings and at the birth of male children. Some engage in prostitution with men, although this is frowned upon. Although there are depictions of alternative genders within Hindu mythology, *hijras* are not revered in the way berdaches were. Indian people are usually uncertain about whether to see *hijras* positively or negatively. However, there appears to be tolerance of their existence as an illustration of the variety present within the universe (Nanda 1994). This challenges Western ways of insisting that sex and gender must entail males being masculine and females being feminine.

Samoan and other Polynesian cultures have also traditionally had a 'third gender', which shows alternative ways of thinking about the relationship between sexed bodies, gender and sexuality (Besnier 1994; Schmidt 2003). Samoan culture understands identity, including gender identity, not as an individual attribute but in terms of a person's position in society and their relation to others in the community. This applies to the third gender, *fa'a-fafine*, who have a recognized position within everyday Samoan life, they work at ordinary jobs, no one really notices them in the supermarket – yet they are men who adopt some feminine ways of being. In the past they took on 'feminine' tasks, usually from an early age, because their family and/or community were short of female labour. As Western ideas have started to have more influence, individual appearance and an emphasis on sexuality have become more important, which is seen by many Samoans as an undesirable shift away from traditional ways (Schmidt 2003). However, as they did traditionally, most *fa'afafine* continue to have a penis; some dress as women and some do not. In any case, both Samoan women and men typically wear *lavalavas* (sarongs) and T-shirts. While *fa'afafine* usually have sex with men, not all do, and there appear to have been cases of *fa'afafine* marrying women and fathering children while continuing to be *fa'afafine*. And the men who have sex with *fa'afafine* continue to be identified as straight men. It is how you have sex, not what type of body you have that is seen as more important. So *fa'afafine* tend to adopt passive, or 'feminine', roles within sex. This further illustrates that what you do, both in terms of labour and the sex act, and not sexed bodies, is key for many cultures in identifying your gender.

Gender variations within cultures

Even where cultures do have a two-sex model, this does not mean that they all share the same expectations about what women and men can and should do. One example is the expectations about women's strength. In Britain, much of Europe, and the rest of 'the West', it is believed that women are physically weak, although this has applied more to middle-class than working-class women. As the sociologist Ann Oakley (1972) suggested back in the 1970s, this is not a belief that other cultures seem to share and indeed in many cultures throughout Africa and Asia, and in some traditional European peasant cultures, women have done most of the carrying of heavy burdens. At the end of the twentieth century, for example, women in Albania were still doing a considerable amount of heavy physical work, even when pregnant. Western researchers have continued to be concerned about this (Senturia 1997), but as Oakley (1972) pointed out more than 30 years ago, the notion that women are frail and delicate does not seem to be borne out by looking at the hard work they routinely perform every day in many parts of the world.

Within Western societies the expectations about women's strength can also vary considerably, according to the context in which that strength is being used. There tends to be considerable public concern about women engaging in 'manly' pursuits such as soldiering, construction work, boxing or body building (Butler 1992; Hargreaves 1997; Pringle and Winning 1998; Brace-Govan 2004). However, female nurses and nurses' aides routinely lift heavy patients (Eriksen *et al.* 2004). This is perhaps seen as acceptable because they are using physical strength within a job that fulfils gender expectations about women as good at caring for others. There are also variations on other deeply held beliefs about gender and sexuality.

Western cultures, at least since the eighteenth century, have believed that women are sexually passive, while men are always struggling to control their sexual appetites. In contrast, in Muslim cultures, there are a variety of ideas and practices around sexuality, but the dominant ideas taken from Islam present women as highly sexual:

> Both women's and men's sexuality are seen as naturally active, and while men's arousal pattern is faster, 'foreplay' is enjoined as a religious duty on men as women also have a desire for and right to sexual pleasure and satisfaction. Women are thought to have a greater potential for sexual desire and pleasure, nine times that of men. However, it is women's passive exudation [giving off] of sexuality to which men are vulnerable, which provokes men who then deliberately arouse and fulfil desire in women. Thus women's sexuality is seen as naturally both greater and more passive than that of men.
>
> (Imam 2000: 122)

Compare this to the widely held opinion, often expressed by the medical profession in Victorian Britain, that women had no sexual desire. As one doctor put it:

> Love of home, children and domestic duties, are the only passions they [women] feel. As a general rule, a modest woman seldom desires any sexual gratification for herself. She submits to her husband, but only to please him . . .
>
> (Acton, cited in Lewis 1984: 126)

Ideas about women's sexuality have clearly changed since the nineteenth century, but there are those who still argue that in the West there remains a double standard that means people tolerate men who are free with their sexual favours, while condemning women (see Duggan and Hunter 2006). Some studies, however, suggest that young people are trying to resist these ways of being sexual and that many girls are now perhaps more able to say they are interested in sex, while boys can say they want love (Allen 2003). Even if women are now more comfortable about being sexually active, this is a very recent thing in the West and we should not assume that Western women are necessarily more 'liberated' in every way than women in non-Western cultures.

People are inclined to be **ethnocentric**, which means that they tend to think that the way things are done in their culture is the 'natural', the best, or the only way to do things. It is all too easy to look at the lives and practices of people in other countries and see them as exotic or even weird, but part of thinking sociologically is to try to see what might be 'weird' about your own culture. It is important to attempt to get some distance in order to see clearly how things, like sex/gender, are done and how they might be done differently. Seeing the strange in the familiar (Berger 1966/1963) is a crucial part of critical sociological thinking. Being critical does not mean simply being negative, but engaging with ideas and practices and thinking about their strengths and limitations.

BEING CRITICAL OF SEXING

There is still considerable scientific debate about to what extent women's and men's bodies (including their brains) are different and how this might relate to their behaviour. The most influential theory of recent years seems to be that of neuroscientist Simon Le Vay (1991). Le Vay is concerned with part of the brain called the hypothalamus, which controls basic operations of the body like breathing, circulation, metabolism and sexual behaviour. He argues that a portion of the hypothalamus, known as part three of the nuclei of the anterior hypothalamus (INAH3), is smaller in women and gay men than in straight men, and others have also found the INAH3 to be bigger in heterosexual males than in heterosexual females (Byne *et al.* 2001). Potentially this difference is thought to account for differences in how women and homo-sexual men's brains develop after birth, and in sexual orientation and behaviour. However, other studies suggest that these proposed differences in the hypothalamus are far from clear (Swaab *et al.* 1995). Le Vay's ideas remain controversial and his early work has been criticized for being based on a small sample (41) of cadavers who died of AIDS. The assumptions he made about their sexuality were guesses, as they were in other key studies (e.g. Byne *et al.* 2001). Le Vay assumed that the drug users were heterosexual and the non-users were homosexual. Also, others who have looked at his data say that the differences between the hypothalamus of women and gay men and the hypothalamus of straight men were not as clear as he presented them to be. His work is thought not to be based closely enough on the evidence. He is said to speculate a great deal, relying on fairly common-sense stereotypes which imply that homosexual men will behave in 'feminine' ways and lesbians will be 'masculine'. He reinforces rather than questions everyday ideas about the relationship between sex/gender/sexuality and ways of behaving (Hird 2004: 30–32). Sometimes such problems are the result of trying to translate intricate technical findings into terms that non-scientists can understand. Scientists are usually very careful about the claims they make, but everyday interpretations of science constantly suggest that women's and men's different biologies make them suited to different tasks.

You can argue that separating out women and men, and saying that they are 'naturally' good at different things, is useful. Even if you think that men and women have learned their capabilities, it can be seen as useful for society if they fulfil different purposes. Functionalists such as Talcott Parsons (see Parsons and Bales 1956) have certainly suggested that the different 'jobs' women and men usually do help keep society running smoothly. He argues that while the men fulfil the instrumental role of going out and being goal orientated and competitive, women can stay at home and focus on the expressive role of caring for their families. The problem with Parsons' view is that it is based on a view of the housewife/breadwinner nuclear family (mum, dad and the children) as the usual and the best way to organize the tasks that need doing in order to survive and to reproduce the next generation. In fact, this is a family form that is very culturally and historically specific to middle-class mid-twentieth-century America. In other times and cultures both mothers and fathers have usually had to work outside the home in order for the family to survive. Also, Parsons does not adequately explain – if both roles are important – why it is the tasks that men do that usually have the most rewards attached in terms of money and prestige. In other words, he has not considered the inequalities that can result from the way society is organized, and how this social environment shapes our bodies as well as what we do.

When people talk about how testosterone makes men aggressive, or the hormones associated with menstruation make women irrational, they are forgetting that the way we live has effects on our bodies. It is not simply a matter of our sexed bodies determining who we are, nearly all the things that we do 'make' our bodies, and in gendered ways.

The social construction of bodies

The different jobs women and men do shape their bodies in different ways. For example, men are much more likely to work in jobs requiring heavy lifting and use of muscle strength, such as construction or road works (Charles and Grusky 2004). Men doing this work will maintain and/or increase a muscular build. Women are usually not thought capable of heavy manual work, but those who do it will also develop muscular builds. That women are capable of developing big muscles can be seen by looking at women bodybuilders. Such women are usually found troubling because they upset our ideas about 'natural' differences between men and women (Mansfield and McGinn 1993), but they show that many sex/gender differences might be a result of how we use our bodies in everyday life.

If it is the case that there are differences in women's and men's brains, it is possible that these are also reinforced, or even developed, because of the different kinds of tasks women and men do in their lives. For example, a relatively recent study of London cab drivers, who are predominantly male, found that they had bigger than average hippocampi. The hippocampus is a part of the brain used for memory and for spatial navigation, and humans have two each. Cab drivers in London have to remember a great deal of information about the roads around London and navigate the shortest route from one place to another. They have to pass a rigorous test on this, called 'the knowledge'. Now it could be that those who already have big hippocampi are more likely to pass the test, but it is also possible that their job might mean that they develop their hippocampi because they use that area of the brain so much (Maguire *et al.* 2000). So the different jobs women and men still tend to do may account for apparent differences in the structure of women's and men's brains.

Also, even if women and men might use their brains differently, this does not mean that one way is better. For example, there is some evidence that men and women use different areas of their brain in working through intellectual problems. However, this does not seem to significantly affect the outcome. Women and men of the same abilities appear to achieve the same standard of intelligence even if they seem to be using different methods (Haier *et al.* 2005). And it is not just manual and mental work that alters our bodies, but a whole range of practices related to bodies, from how we eat to how we dress.

Take wearing high-heeled shoes, which can have considerable impact on women's bodies. They help draw sexual attention to women by forcing them to walk with their breasts and their bottoms pushed out in order to balance. The posture is one that men may find erotic as it emphasizes a woman's 'womanly' features. However, it can cause problems. High heels might restrict women's ability to move, not only when wearing them but resulting in long-term injuries that impair mobility. Walking in high-heeled shoes puts twice as much force on women's joints as walking barefoot (McBride *et al.* 1991). High heels contribute to shin splints and deform the pelvis. They make it hard for women to run away if in danger (Stanley 1995: 133, 172). Although many movies might show us active, powerful women performing amazing feats in stilettos, one has to wonder how realistic that is and, if it is, what kind of damage they might be doing to their feet and back! High heels are but one example of a wide range of practices that reinforce ideals about gender in ways that actually alter bodies. It may seem a fairly frivolous example, but this is a book about everyday life and it is good to think about how even the most everyday decision about what kind of shoes we wear can contribute to the forming of gendered bodies.

SUMMARY

Two sexes are not enough to describe the variety found among human beings. And what exactly makes someone 'male' or 'female'? Is it having a penis or vagina, having particular chromosomes or genes? Is it thinking differently, or having different strength or amounts of bodily hair? Do any of these things matter in how we live our everyday lives? In this chapter, such questions were answered by looking at how understandings of sex (female/ male) have changed, and at other cultures' ways of thinking about sex/gender divisions. A rigid division of bodies into 'female' or 'male' tends to be used to justify inequalities that result from the way society is organized. Our everyday lives are not simply determined by whether we have a male or female body, but ideas about what kinds of abilities men and women have can limit the kind of things we do. And the kinds of tasks we do and the practices, such as dressing and eating, that we engage in shape our bodies. If women and men are usually doing different kinds of things then they are liable to end up with different kinds of bodies. In this sense, sexed bodies are used as the basis for deciding what kinds of things a person 'should' be able to do. If women pursue what are considered 'feminine' pursuits and men go about being 'masculine', then this will reinforce the idea that gendered ways of acting are caused by sexed bodies. However, it may often be the case that doing 'feminine' things makes a body appear 'womanly' and that 'masculine' deeds produce 'manly' bodies. It is clear from looking at historical change, cultural variations and thinking critically, that the everyday social world plays a big part in how we inhabit our gendered bodies.

2

LEARNING AND DOING GENDER IN EVERYDAY LIFE

INTRODUCTION

> Several persons were prominent in [Agnes's] accounts with whom she not only acted like a lady but learned, from them, how to act like a lady. An important partner instructor was [her boyfriend] Bill's mother in whose home she spent a great deal of time as a prospective daughter-in-law. Bill's mother was of Dutch-Indonesian ancestry and supported herself as a dressmaker. While teaching Agnes to cook Dutch dishes to please Bill, she also taught Agnes how to cook in the first place. Agnes said that Bill's mother taught her dressmaking and materials; she taught her which clothes she should wear; they discussed dress shops, shopping, styles that were appropriate for Agnes, and the skills of home management.
>
> (Garfinkel 1967: 146)

This is a description of a young American woman in the late 1950s, learning from her future mother-in-law everyday things that will make her a 'good wife'. We can recognize Agnes learning the kinds of skills and characteristics that, at the time, were thought essential for being feminine, 'ladylike'. This could be any young woman learning from her elders. What is unusual is that Agnes spent the first 17 years of her life living as a boy. Harold Garfinkel encounters Agnes in his work at the gender clinic at the University of California, Los Angeles (UCLA), where he, as a social psychologist/sociologist, and a team of medical and psychiatric personnel headed by Robert Stoller were doing research on people who do not fit neatly into one of the two socially approved sex/gender categories. Agnes was born with a penis and a scrotum, and was identified as male and raised accordingly. When Garfinkel met her at age 19, she still had a penis, but also had a feminine body shape, including large breasts which had developed at puberty (Garfinkel reveals how this happened in an appendix to his book *Studies in Ethnomethodology*). Until the age of 17 everyone had recognized and treated Agnes as a boy. Then:

> [a]fter considerable planning, rehearsals, dieting to 'make myself pretty,' and similar preparations, she left her home town in August 1956 for a month's visit with a grandmother in Midwest City. At the end of the month's visit, according to plan, she left her grandmother's house without leaving word of her whereabouts, and in a downtown hotel changed to feminine attire with the hope of finding a job in that city.
>
> (Garfinkel 1967: 120)

Two years later, Agnes met Bill and moved to the San Fernando Valley to be closer to him; shortly afterwards she was seen for the first time at UCLA, meeting weekly to talk to Garfinkel until and after a castration operation was performed and a vagina constructed. What is interesting for sociologists about Agnes is that she illustrates how gender is something that we learn to do and can relearn, although this may not be easy:

> Agnes vehemently insisted that she was, and was to be treated as, a natural, normal female. . . . While her claims to her natural femininity could be advanced they could not be taken for granted. Many matters

> [such as initial problems with her constructed vagina] served as
> obstinate reminders that her femininity, though claimed, could be
> claimed only at the cost of vigilance and work.
>
> (Garfinkel 1967: 134)

The only real difference between Agnes and other women is that
Agnes had to learn how to do femininity rather late in life, and was
more conscious of how she did things and more worried about
getting it 'wrong' than most women. This process of learning to
do gender has to take account of what kind of body you have, but
is not determined by it.

If sex refers to basic bodily differences (female/male) that interest biologists, gender refers to how people learn about how to be
feminine or masculine and apply what they learn in living their
everyday lives. **Socialization** is the process by which we learn how
to act appropriately as members of a particular society. What is
thought 'appropriate' for girls and women, as compared to boys
and men, often differs. A major part of socialization is about
learning how to do gender. **Social structure**, the way society is
organized (for example, around classes), is crucial in shaping our
actions in gendered ways. Crucial in forming gender is the way
families are established and who does what within them. Other
institutions, such as the education system and the mass media, are
key **agents of socialization**: they are central in how people learn
to do gender. Also important is the way that a particular society
organizes for the everyday work to be done that is needed to keep
things running. Who is most suited to different kinds of work is
often decided partly according to gender. Not only social structure
but ideas about 'femininity' or 'masculinity' shape people. It is not
just being born with a penis that makes you masculine, and in
fact we sometimes describe people with male bodies ('men') as
'feminine'.

Sociologists argue that what is meant by 'feminine' and
'masculine' is not fixed, and depends on the way a particular society has of understanding gender at a particular time. In other

words, **gender is socially constructed**. It can be shown that gender is socially constructed by using the sociological imagination to explore how gender has meant different things and been done differently in different times and places. A look at history illustrates changing ways of learning and doing gender. Then there is a comparison of different ways of doing gender within present everyday life. Here, rather than look at how different cultures have different ways of doing gender, examples of varieties of styles of masculinity and femininity within contemporary Western culture are examined. The rest of the chapter focuses on attempts within sociology to critically understand gender, not as 'natural', but as done within the everyday lives of individuals. If gender is learned and done, it can be done differently, and perhaps in ways more likely to promote equality.

HISTORIES OF DOING GENDER

Working at gender

What it means to be feminine or masculine has altered throughout history. This tends to be ignored in common-sense thinking, which imagines that there are long-standing traditional ways of being a woman or a man that reflect what is 'natural' and therefore should not be changed. In relation to femininity it is thought that women's traditional or 'natural' role is as mothers and that they should devote all or most of their attention to this and not work. However, this is based on the idea that 'work' is something done outside the home and that what women do as housewives and mothers does not count as work. That women's 'natural' role means not doing paid work can be challenged by looking at what women have done in the past. Prior to Europe's Industrial Revolution in the eighteenth century, for example, the vast majority of women were centrally engaged in the business of helping their families survive. The work this involved often took place in or near the home. Most of the population lived in rural areas and women helped work the land, with even young children joining in with whatever tasks they were able to do. Some families worked together in craft industries such as weaving. Usually the women did the spinning, the men the weaving, and children assisted with the carding of wool and housework. But there were some divisions between work done at home and out in the wider public world, and even then women were involved. In the medieval period in Britain, for example, women worked in a wide range of occupations. However, women's relationship to work began to change:

> In the guilds their situation was being progressively weakened. The old protections and privileges of widows disappeared, and as apprenticeships became more formal the entrance of women to trades was closed. A sustained struggle developed from the sixteenth century over the definition of 'women's work'. Some trades which had been reserved for women were encroached upon and eventually taken over by men. Brewing was probably originally a women's trade but by the seventeenth century brewsters (female brewers) were prohibited. In York, despite women's resistance, men replaced them in candlemaking.
>
> (Rowbotham 1972: 26)

This may be a picture of past women's lives that is slightly surprising if we think that there has been steady and clear progress from women being dependent on men and under their thumbs, to some present situation of independence. It also contradicts common-sense ideas which sometimes assume that women were previously stay-at-home housewives and have only recently gone out to 'work'. It is important to note that there are always a variety of social expectations about and ways of doing femininity and masculinity at a particular time, they are always changing and are open to being interpreted and challenged by individuals.

The eighteenth century is a period which illustrates well that there were constantly changing and sometimes competing ways of doing masculinity. During the 1700s in Britain there was a shift away from earlier characterizations of the ideal man as the honourable head of the household in control of his dependents, towards an ideal of the polite gentleman. This meant men of the social elites paying attention to their dress and cultivating charming manners. Some styles of polite masculinity were thought to take this 'too far' and there was considerable criticism by their contemporaries of groups like the Fops and the Macaronis, who some thought to be rather too 'feminine' in their dress and manners (Harvey 2005). But there were also men who presented themselves in ways more familiar to us as 'manly' – they are the men you see in paintings called 'the hunt' or 'a sportsman'. Usually there are guns involved, often horses, and lots of dogs. Unlike polite gentlemen, these men like the outdoors and prefer to avoid the society of women (see Davidoff and Hall 1987). One example is Ann's brother-in-law Charles, in Jane Austen's novel *Persuasion*. Meanwhile, most ordinary menfolk are toiling away in a hard life on the land. This begins to change as Europe industrializes and much of the population shifts from country to city living.

During the nineteenth century, industrialization forces people to take up entirely new ways of surviving, which have huge implications for how women and men live and act. For those working in the new factories and living in the terrible conditions of the rapidly expanding manufacturing towns, there is a period where many continue to work as a family unit with the husband in charge. However, women and children were much sought after on their own because they could be paid less. Eventually, the situation where families worked together in the factories became uncommon due to technological changes and to new laws restricting children's hours. Then followed laws restricting women's hours, which reflected concerns, among working-class men and upper-class reformers, about who is caring for children and tending to home life. These concerns were convenient for working-class men, who benefited from being able to compete for work more easily and from having greater control over more dependent families once women's and children's ability to earn was limited (Hartmann 1976). These concerns were in part the product of upper-class Victorian ideas about women as delicate and angelic, which were related to new ideas about children, not as small adults who must help work for the family, but as innocent cherubs who should be cosseted (Aries 1962). While traces of these ideas remain, new ways of learning and doing gender have emerged since the nineteenth century.

Models of femininity and masculinity

There has been a great deal of debate about the increasing influence of the mass media on how children, and indeed adults, learn and do gender. We usually think of movies, television and magazines when we think of mass media (and I will discuss some of them shortly), but there are other sources that have provided guidance on appropriate behaviour for both sexes, and these show how what is considered 'appropriate' changes. Dutch sociologist Cas Wouters looked at etiquette books of the twentieth century, which contained advice on good manners. He argues that these illustrate how social distance and formality between women and men has decreased in the last 100 years or so (see Wouters 1995). For example, a Dutch author around 1910 comments on how rules about dances have changed:

> Fifteen years ago it would have been completely unnecessary to say anything about dancing in public. Ladies and young girls from good families did not dream of exhibiting their talents anywhere but at invitation balls. Public dance halls were for soldiers and servant-girls.
>
> (cited in Wouters 1995: 327)

However, in the 1920s there were still fairly strict notions about under what conditions young men and women could get to know each other, as this English author warns:

> When any gentleman, newly introduced to a girl, has escorted her home from the scene of the introduction, it is not correct for her to ask him to call, or for him to seek the permission from her. Any such invitation must come from the girl's mother, or any friends with whom she may be staying, so if she wishes to see more of her cavalier, she should introduce him to her mother or hostess.
>
> (cited in Wouters 1995: 328)

And even by the 1980s etiquette books still give a clear idea that the social expectations of women are that they will be wives and mothers and men will be breadwinners (at least temporarily). Advice given reflects these ideas about gender, although equality is creeping in:

> The person who issues the invitation pays. Usually he pays for her. His payment is for the pleasure of her company – nothing more . . . If he is courting her he should pay. One day she will become pregnant or give up work temporarily to look after their under-fives and she needs to know that he is able and willing to pay for two – even three.
>
> (cited in Wouters 1995: 331)

Such advice on how to act in social situations tells us a great deal about changing ways of doing gender. Talking to parents and grandparents can reveal similar changes. Your older relatives might inform you that 'in their day' young women were not allowed out in 'that' kind of clothing, or that men knew how to treat women 'properly'. These are people trying to explain their discomfort with current ways of doing gender and they may also complain about what they see in the media.

Portrayals of femininity in women's magazines have provided a popular source for sociologists and feminists analysing ideas about gender that were current in particular historical periods (e.g. McRobbie 1991; Walker 1998). Betty Friedan's (1965) famous book *The Feminine Mystique* is one example. She argued that the media were highly influential in promoting traditional ways of doing femininity. She proposed that, in 1950s America, magazines played a key role in making women believe that being feminine meant devoting your life to being a stay-at-home housewife and mother. Women were told that it was performing this role that would bring them satisfaction. That was 'the feminine mystique'. However, in talking to some women in the early 1960s Friedan discovered that many housewives were far from satisfied, but did not know how to express what ailed them. This was what she called 'the problem with no name'. Middle-class educated women, isolated out in the newly formed suburban landscapes of America, found themselves bored and depressed. Under these conditions, the housewife role was restrictive rather than satisfying, but it was very difficult for the women to say they were unhappy because then they were in danger of being thought 'unwomanly'. Friedan's solution was not very radical – she recommended that individual women make changes to their lives to pursue their own interests more – but her identification of the problem was important for a whole generation of women in being able to make choices. It allowed many women to imagine, and to find, alternative ways of doing femininity that they found more fulfilling. Many people credit her book as vital in prompting the feminist movement of the 1960s, one key element of which was to be critical of the way that women were represented in the media.

There have been many other studies about the media, but questions have remained about just how much influence the media have on how women and men act. It is not easy to determine whether they produce gender stereotypes, or just reflect current ideas about how to do gender (see Gauntlett 2002). Media images are often criticized for being unrealistic portrayals, and harmful if 'real' women and men try to live up to them (for example, by starving themselves) (e.g. Bordo 1989). However, the media can also portray more diverse ways of doing gender than many people might experience in their everyday lives (Van Zoonen 1995). The TV show *Queer Eye for the Straight Guy* or the movie *Brokeback Mountain*, for example, might make people think differently about masculinity and find new ways of being a man. There are varying explanations of how these processes of learning and doing gender might operate.

CLASS COMPARISONS: LEARNING GENDER DIFFERENTLY

In contemporary society different men and women learn and do their gender in diverse ways, but sociologists look for patterns that explain why certain groups of people might do gender in similar ways. The way that people do gender depends on the different situations they are in, but also on their location within society. People who come from similar backgrounds and are of similar ages will probably learn and do things in similar ways. As well as cultural background – for example, being Samoan, Greek or Thai (see Chapter 1) – the **class** (see Introduction) you belong to will be crucial in determining how you express femininity or masculinity and what kinds of gendered behaviour the people around you think is appropriate. French sociologist Pierre Bourdieu (see Skeggs 1997) has been influential in trying to explain how ways of being and doing become ingrained. He uses the term **habitus** to refer to how what we think and do and like, and how we dress and talk are learned within particular class backgrounds and become habits that form who we are. Class hierarchies are perpetuated by the way people use these ways of being and doing things to distinguish themselves as 'better' than people lower down the social scale. Class habitus also involves particular ways of doing gender.

Usually, middle- and upper-class ways of doing gender are valued more within society. There are various sociologists who have done good work on this – R.W. Connell's (1995) Australian-based investigations of *Masculinities*, for example, are excellent. Bev Skeggs (1997) has also illustrated the relationship between class habitus and how gender is done in her research on working-class women in Britain. In their everyday lives these women are constantly struggling with respectability. Ideas about who and what is worthy of respect reinforce class hierarchies. There are always reminders for working-class women that other people think they are worthless. One woman experienced this when working for a middle-class family:

> When I first went to work as a nanny I couldn't stand it. They [the middle-class people] really think they are something else. They treat you like shit. What I've noticed is they never look at you. Well they do at first they look you all over and make you feel like a door rag, but then they just tell you what to do. One of them asked me if I had any other clothes. Some of them want you to know that you are shit in comparison to them.
>
> (quoted in Skeggs 1997: 92)

Skeggs' point is that ideals of femininity are based on middle-class ways of being and doing 'womanliness'. Working-class women may find middle-class women snobby and pretentious, but know that if they can try to appear to be respectably feminine they might be able to get 'better' jobs, 'better' men and 'better' lives. Another working-class woman explains the everyday struggles, for example over dress, that this involves:

> All the time you've got to weigh everything up: is it too tarty? Will I look like a right slag in it what will people think? It drives me mad that every time you go to put your clothes on you have to think 'do I look dead common? Is it rough? Do I look like a dog?'
>
> (Skeggs 1997: 3)

Britain is often characterized as a particularly class-bound society, but even in the supposedly meritocratic United States of America similar kinds of devaluations of working-class femininity operate. One illustration of this can be seen in media coverage of one of the sex scandals in which previous president Bill Clinton was involved around 1998 (Holmes 2000a). At that time a woman called Paula Jones claimed that when Clinton was Governor of Arkansas he had sexually harassed her. She was working for him and allegedly he invited her to what she thought was a meeting and then exposed himself to her and suggested they engage in sexual activity. She declined and, some years later, when he was President, she laid a formal complaint. Jones found it hard to get her complaint taken seriously. She was discredited by being called 'trailer park trash, a loose woman' (Romano, cited in Holmes 2000a: 313). Her appearance was criticized, she was thought to not be believable because of her working-class hairstyle and clothes. So with the help of supporters interested in politically harming Clinton, Jones altered her bodily appearance to try to make her 'respectable'. Her hair was made straighter and 'smaller'. She changed her make-up to 'natural, not neon, hues' and started to dress like she came from 'the boardroom instead of the secretarial pool'. To some extent these 'markers of dignity, refinement and power' helped her to be taken more seriously, confirming that 'there is potent politics in a haircut and a well-chosen shade of lipstick' (Givhan, cited in Holmes 2000a: 313). Such 'markers of dignity, refinement and power' are based on middle-class ways of doing gender. The 'professional' boardroom suit is understood as indicating a desexualized competent woman who is very different to the working-class secretary in 'tarty' skirts. However, wearing a suit is not enough to free women from sexual objectification, nor does it automatically make them powerful. Jones's case did not proceed to court and Clinton remained in power (Holmes 2000a). It remains difficult for people to escape the ways of doing gender that they have learned within their class background. Trying to understand how gender is learned, rather than natural, has been central to social science attempts to think critically about our everyday world and how it might be changed.

CRITICAL EVALUATIONS OF HOW GENDER IS LEARNT AND DONE

While there was some attention to women's social position by sociologists prior to the 1970s (see Sydie 1987; Delamont 1990:

139–159; Hill and Hoecker-Drysdale 2001), this work, much of it by women, is largely overlooked in histories of sociology. When what is now known as the sociology of gender began to emerge in the 1970s women sociologists therefore had to begin again in trying to understand what role society plays in shaping women and men. British sociologist Ann Oakley's book *Sex, Gender and Society* (1972) was instrumental in these renewed attempts to understand gender as something not natural, but learned.

Gender socialization: learning gender

Oakley (1972) argues that people learn the 'normal' ways to act feminine or masculine in their society through **socialization** processes. She borrowed the term 'gender' from the 1960s work of Robert Stoller, the psychiatrist mentioned above, who was working – at the University of California, Los Angeles – on gender identity and intersex people (see Jackson 1998). She argues that early socialization of children within the family is especially important in teaching people to act in ways thought appropriate for their gender. As soon as a baby is born people treat it differently and expect it to act differently depending on whether it is a girl or a boy. Girls tend to be treated as, and expected to be, more delicate and dependent, while boys are treated as, and thought to be, more robust and independent. Oakley says that this different treatment has huge effects on how children come to act.

As the American sociologist Jessie Bernard (e.g. 1981) put it, everyday life – especially for children under five – is divided into a 'pink world' for girls and a 'blue world' for boys. The pink world is one that encourages girls to be passive and emotional, and the blue world expects boys to be independent and active. A literal example of the division between pink and blue worlds can be seen if you go into the nearest shop selling children's clothes and/or toys. Look for large groupings of pink and that will be where you will find the clothing intended for girls. And, in a less literal sense, the pink and blue worlds are reinforced in the toy section where vacuum cleaners, tea sets and dolls like real babies can be bought to reinforce ideas of femininity as about being a wife and mother who cares for others. Meanwhile, trains and tool sets and heroic action figures present a masculine life as one orientated around active work and adventure.

Although socialization is important, often those who write about it focus too much on the influence of parents and especially mothers (Stanley and Wise 1983). Oakley, for example, does note that children make judgements about gender expectations partly by comparing their parents to other people, but keeps returning to what mothers do with children. Yet it is clear that a range of people apart from parents communicate messages to young children about how to be a girl or be a boy. It is hard to know how influential these other sources might be. Ideas about socialization also seem to assume that the 'lessons' about how to be feminine or masculine are clear and that children passively take them on. However, there are many, often contradictory, messages about gender that children have to choose between (Stanley and Wise 1983). They learn about different ways to act feminine or masculine from their extended family, their friends, at childcare, school, from books, movies and television. And although the first five years are crucial in shaping someone's gender identity, gender socialization is a process that continues throughout our life.

Families are crucial in the gender socialization of children, but schools have become increasingly important since education was made compulsory (around the 1870s in most Western countries). In the 1970s there was a lot of concern about girls not achieving as well at school as boys. Some researchers argued that this was because girls were given less attention in the classroom (Spender 1982) or because learning materials like reading and textbooks reinforced stereotypes about girls as stupid and passive, and did not appeal to girls' interests (e.g. Lobban 1975). However, others have suggested that the school environment is very middle-class and feminine, and that this puts working-class kids off education (see Connell *et al.* 1982). Paul Willis's (1977) famous study,

Learning to Labour, was an analysis of why working-class boys did so badly in 1970s English schools. These boys associated school-work with femininity, and preserving their image of toughness meant not being good at schoolwork. Boys who were good academically were 'cissies'. Most of this early work assumes that girls and boys take on ideas about gender that are forced upon them by the school, the teachers, or the way their world is already organized. It seems that the children do not have much choice about how they do their gender. However, more recent work shows how children often play a quite active part in deciding between the options available (Davies 1993; Thorne 1993).

Barrie Thorne's (1993) study of American elementary (primary) school children illustrates how gender is something that children experiment with as they learn about it. R.W. Connell (2002: 12–16) gives a good summary of her research. Thorne notes that gender difference is not always being enforced – for example, in the classroom the key division is often between pupils and teacher. In some of the games in the playground, however, children do work at making clear 'borders' between girls and boys – for example, groups of girls will chase groups of boys according to often quite elaborate rules about where girls or boys can and cannot go and what they can do. This is one example of how sociologists see gender as governed by social rules.

Symbolic interactionism: doing gender

To say that there are social rules about doing gender challenges common-sense understandings of gender as naturally hardwired into us. People may take gender for granted most of the time, but it is something that we put effort into doing. **Symbolic interactionism** argues that gender is learnt and done within interaction. Garfinkel's (1967) work in the 1950s and 1960s, mentioned above, was some of the earliest, and he established the idea of gender as a managed achievement. He was an **ethnomethodologist**, so was interested in how the way people understand their world determines how they act within it. For Garfinkel, social rules about gender understand people as 'naturally' coming in two types: feminine women and masculine men. Agnes was putting considerable effort into 'passing' as a feminine woman, especially when she still had a penis. However, it is not only Agnes, but 'normal' women who try to act 'ladylike'. Think of all the time many women spend trying to make themselves 'more feminine' by removing body hair, applying make-up, dressing with care. And men might put considerable effort into being 'manly', working out at the gym to build their muscles, biting back tears so as not to appear emotional. However, unless they are transsexuals, most people tend not to spend much time worrying about getting it 'wrong' when doing gender. At least they know that there is considerable leeway in how to be 'feminine' or 'masculine'. So girls might climb trees and women might now fight in the army, and although these actions might be thought 'unladylike' and masculine, people do not suddenly decide that those who do them must 'really' be men. Yet although the rules might be bent, this does not mean that people can do anything they like. Garfinkel talks about Agnes's fear of breaking the social rules about gender; she knows that there are likely to be consequences: humiliation and ostrasization, for example. And this is true for 'normals'. For example, Western women who do not remove their leg or underarm hair are likely to be made fun of and/or stigmatized as 'lesbians' (and why that is thought an insult is another story). Garfinkel tends to focus on what Agnes did to 'pass' as a woman. Aspects of this were like being an undercover agent – for example, if she went swimming she had to wear tight underwear and a bathing suit with a skirt to disguise her penis. However, Agnes *insisted* that she was naturally female, that her penis was an accident and like a wart that needed to be removed. Like those with less confusing biology, she engaged in ongoing actions to try to present herself as a natural woman. She may have been more aware of needing to manage risk and uncertainty so that she was not 'found out', but all of us take part in routines that reinforce the social rules about how to do gender.

When we meet people in everyday life we present ourselves in gendered ways and we look at how other people present themselves so that we know how to interact. From the clothing people wear, their hairstyle, tone of voice and other cues we decide on their gender and this will influence whether we flirt or talk about sport, or are surprised when they say they are a nuclear physicist, and so on. Erving Goffman (1979) provides an analysis of everyday routines of interacting in his book *The Presentation of Self in Everyday Life* (Goffman 1987/1959). In that early work he set out his ideas about social interaction as like a drama in which we are actors. We play a part, and he argued that we change how we play that part depending on our audience. People try to present themselves to advantage – say, taking the role of the dutiful granddaughter when with the grandparents, but being a rather wild party girl when out with friends. Gender is crucial in how those situations are set up in ways that make us play our role according to **social scripts** about being feminine or masculine (Goffman 1979). When we interact with others, there are various displays we use to indicate who is involved in the interaction, how they might act, think, feel, and what they might expect. **Displays** are mostly non-verbal forms of behaviour, which are very structured in ways that determine how we interact with people. Most displays take the form of bracket rituals: they establish the start and end of interactions. So, for example, men used to stand up when a woman entered the room. This was based on, and set up, a whole series of beliefs about women as in need of men's chivalry. Although seen as respectful, this reinforced ideas that men were protectors and women in need of protection. Gender displays also involve certain styles of dress, appearance and talking, which identify who is to be dealt with.

Goffman (1979) is critical of how gender displays tend to be based upon and used to confirm current social expectations about men as 'naturally' dominant and women as subordinate. Displays reinforce that gender hierarchy as 'natural'. Sometimes these are stylized, so that the display is rather exaggerated. One example might be a man flexing his muscles before lifting a heavy box for a woman. People have some choice about whether or not to engage in some of these displays. It is not necessarily the case that women will need or appreciate men's help with lifting boxes, and men may not always offer it. If they do they might make fun of the whole thing, the muscle flexing might be a joke intended to show that the man does not think that he is macho and the woman is weak and fragile. However, some men might sincerely offer their help in such situations. Although there are variations, when all these gender displays are analysed it is possible to see a pattern which perpetuates the notion that women and men are not equal. Goffman (1979) illustrates this by looking at advertisements. In these he argues that women are displayed as smaller, and as passive. Men are shown as there to protect and guide them. Although many individual women are taller than a good number of the men around them, when taller women are pictured next to shorter men the intent is often to make people laugh or to indicate something 'unnatural'. The advertisements present images of men as strong, while women are pictured as childlike and fragile. People see this constantly and therefore think that it is 'natural'. Goffman argues that gender is not 'natural' but an illusion created in interaction with others. In those interactions women and men follow scripts that set out how women and men are expected to act, but like actors in a play they have some freedom to interpret the scripts and do things a little differently. Goffman's ideas are very useful, but not without some problems.

People are very concerned to manage how others might see them, but Garfinkel (1967: 173–175) questions just how 'deliberate' or calculated this impression management is when it comes to gender. Goffman assumes that people deliberately 'con' others, trying to present themselves in the best light. It is true that for Agnes to be recognized as a woman requires her to lie and to do things a certain way. Her need to manage how she presents herself might be especially pressing because she (at first) has to hide her 'male' genitals and her childhood as a boy. However, everyone has to manage their gender presentation and this often involves covering things up. Sometimes we are required to do certain things to be seen as a 'normal' woman. For example, a woman might hide her unshaved legs in order not to be subject to ridicule. Another woman might cover up her dislike for children because the expectation is that women are 'naturally' maternal and nurturing, so she might be thought 'unwomanly' and possibly even not a nice person. Men wear trousers, not because they are necessarily trying to look more manly but because it is not usually acceptable for them to wear skirts (unless they are Fijian or Scottish, and then particular traditional versions of a 'skirt' are permissible). People may want to break these rules but fear what will happen if they do. They are not 'deliberately' lying, but their choices about how they present themselves are constrained by social rules, especially rules about gender. However, as Garfinkel (1967: 173–175) claims, Goffman's understanding of how people follow rules is too concerned with particular episodes, rather than with how people build on past experiences and adapt them to new situations. Garfinkel's work is built on by other ethnomethodologists and heirs to symbolic interactionism. They were keen to emphasize the point that gender is something we *continue* to learn about and to work at doing.

People create a world in which there are two, and only two, genders, and act according to that belief. This is the main insight of Suzanne Kessler and Wendy McKenna (1985/1978), who share Garfinkel's ethnomethodological approach but give a more detailed analysis of how we learn and do gender. They suggest that even where someone's sex/gender is unclear or confusing people will make a decision about which gender they are and treat them accordingly. Kessler and McKenna (1985/1978) use the term 'gender attribution' to refer to the decisions people make about which gender category to put someone in. For example, transvestites dress in a way that upsets social expectations about what men should wear and what women should wear. However, rather than deciding that cross-dressers are somewhere in between the categories 'female/feminine' and 'male/masculine', people will decide that a drag queen is feminine, or not notice any breasts and be convinced that a 'butch' woman dressed in a suit is 'really' a man. So people might use biological signs like facial hair or breasts to make gender attributions, but these signs do not always reliably demarcate women from men; for example, some 'women' may have facial hair. The key point of what Kessler and McKenna (1985/1978: 17) are saying is that 'whether someone is a woman or a man is determined in the course of interacting'. Once we have decided whether someone is a man or a woman, we are very unlikely to change our minds. Even if someone has a sex change, those around them often struggle to learn to interact with a person who they knew as Paul but is now Rachel. Yet a sex change is not always needed to move into a different gender category. As the story of Agnes prior to her castration suggests, people with a penis may live their lives as 'women'. Some who are biologically mostly female may live their lives as 'men'. What it means to live as a woman or a man is determined by the people with whom we live and interact. Kessler and McKenna (1985/1978) talk mostly about transsexuals, but use them to illustrate the kind of work everybody has to do to continuously maintain gender within everyday interactions.

Gender is therefore about acting the part, but also about looking the part so that others will know how to treat us. When people interact they do so in relation to the other person, taking their cues about what a suitable way of being feminine or masculine might be in that situation. We manage our responses to other people's assessment of our femaleness or maleness. West and Zimmerman (1987) build on the work of other symbolic interactionists to argue this in a rather belatedly published version of ideas about 'doing gender', first presented in the 1970s. Unlike Goffman, they think that gender is a fundamental part of all interactions, not something that just frames the start and finish. Women and men are always drawing on current ideas about how women and men should look and act. And without knowing another person's gender it is almost impossible to interact with them. This suggests that doing gender is not optional, but a required part of our everyday engagement with people. We are all constantly working at presenting ourselves as feminine or masculine in relation to others, and through this interactive work gender is produced. We are always doing gender, sometimes more consciously, but also other people are doing our gender to us. This can be illustrated via a story about a straight male friend of mine who owned a particularly nice pale-blue fluffy jumper. He liked this jumper but reported that whenever he wore it someone would shout 'poofter' at him in the street. He did not mind being thought gay, but it was a reminder that other men felt he was not obeying the rules about 'manly' ways of dressing and they were trying to punish him for upsetting gender boundaries.

The possibility of 'punishment' makes doing gender sound rather precarious and like hard work for individuals to 'get right'. The problem with all symbolic interactionism is that although it suggests that individuals are constrained in how they do gender by the people around them, it puts the emphasis on how actors make choices about doing gender within those constraints. This is thought to be too voluntaristic by other theorists of gender who do not think that we can select how to do gender in the way that we choose what clothes to put on in the morning (Butler 1993: x). The most influential current thinking on gender, by Judith Butler, shares much with the symbolic interactionist approach, but tries to get away from this voluntarism.

Judith Butler: gender makes us the kind of human beings that others understand

Socially constructed ideas about gender can be seen as fundamental in how we understand what a person is and in how people act and how their actions are understood. Judith Butler (e.g. 1990, 1993) is not convinced that gender is a performance in the way symbolic interactionists suggest, but highlights how gender constructs us as subjects (thinking, acting human beings). In this she is perhaps most like Kessler and McKenna, although drawing on a different set of ideas. Like them she sees gender as a social construction that creates the reality in which people live their lives. Like them she thinks that, at birth, people are assigned a gender, based on medical interpretation of whether their bodies are 'male' or 'female'. This then sets up how that person is treated and what are thought appropriate ways for them to act.

When a child is born and the doctors say 'it's a girl' then that child becomes part of a whole social framework in which whatever she does will be understood in relation to ideas about gender. Butler refers to this process as the 'girling' of the girl. Although this sounds similar to socialization theories about learning gender, Butler is saying something a little more radical. Socialization theories assume that people are born as neutral human beings and that they learn their gender, it being written upon them as though they are a blank slate. Butler is saying that we can only understand people as gendered. There is no neutral or in-between category for human beings. People only make sense to us, are only 'culturally intelligible' (Butler 1990: 16–17), if we think about them as girls/women or as boys/men. Ideas about gender therefore make people who they are, but people can play with those ideas in shaping themselves.

For Butler (1990), gender is not something that actors do (as symbolic interactionists suggest), but is a way of thinking about the world that produces people as 'feminine' women or 'masculine' men. The 'choices' a person makes might sometimes reinforce conventional ideas about gender, but it is possible to cause 'gender trouble' – for example, by a man wearing a fluffy pale-blue jumper, or an adult woman climbing a tree or taking up boxing. Butler is saying that gender is something that comes into being by people imitating what they think is appropriate gendered behaviour and that contributes to what we believe about gender. But imitations always differ slightly so they also change how gender operates. In other words, gender is a social construction, something people have made up. If we stop believing that it is natural and realize that it is made up then we can explain how change is possible.

SUMMARY

The kinds of rules that we learn about doing gender might be embedded in social structures and ideas in ways that constrain us, but we are able to make some choices. That certain conventional ways of doing gender are natural can be challenged by looking at the different ways that gender has been done throughout history. And in contemporary everyday life, social structures like class hierarchies produce varying patterns of femininity and masculinity. Comparing these (and other differences such as between cultures) illustrates that some ways of doing gender are valued more than others and that these are passed on in ways that reinforce the power of certain social groups such as middle- and upper-class men.

This all indicates that gender is something that we learn to do. The sociological history of trying to understand gender as an ongoing doing of 'femininity' or 'masculinity' can be traced back to Harold Garfinkel. As a result of working with intersex and transsexual people, Garfinkel realized that 'normal' people were also always engaged in doing their gender, and that gender was a managed achievement. Goffman focused less on the active management of gender and more on the ritual aspects of how gender was established as a relation in interaction. Kessler and McKenna, like Garfinkel, present an ethnomethodological account of gender, which means that they are centrally concerned with how people construct a social reality around their beliefs, in this case the belief that there are only two genders. They provide much more theoretical thinking on the topic than Garfinkel and emphasize much more strongly the point that it is not so much how individuals do their gender, but how all of us make decisions about what gender a person is and interpret their actions according to that decision.

Once we have decided that someone is a man, anything he does will be interpreted as 'normal' for a man, or unusual. If he does something 'feminine' we will see that as an exception not as an indication that he is 'really' a woman. West and Zimmerman draw on both Garfinkel and Goffman to explain the doing of gender as involving considerable work. However, they emphasize the work of an individual woman or man in that doing, and underestimate the work of the others with whom they are interacting. Nevertheless, this important perspective provides key insights into how gender is socially constructed. Our gender is something that we actively do, but it is also something done to us by others. The way a particular society structures family life, work, education, and class and other hierarchies will influence how people do gender, but within these constraints individuals can make some choices for themselves. Those choices will be shaped by what they think about the variety of ideas about gender that are available to them. If people can recognize that gender is not 'natural' but socially constructed, then rather than having others determine how they 'should' behave, people can be more active in changing how gender is done. Maybe we are starting to recognize that we do not need to insist that people are either feminine or masculine. To imagine more, and more fluid, gender categories is to imagine a possible world that might be fairer and more interesting than the present one.

3

GENDERED RELATIONSHIPS IN EVERYDAY LIFE

INTRODUCTION

> Within this vibrant society of people, it's easy to find people with similar interests to you. Once you meet people you like, you find it's easy to communicate and stay in touch.
>
> At any time there are dozens of events where you can party at nightclubs, attend fashion shows and art openings or just play games.
>
> Residents also form groups ranging from neighborhood associations to fans of Sci Fi Movies.
>
> (Linden Research, Inc. 2007)

This might sound a little bit like an advertisement for a holiday destination for young people. In fact it is from information about meeting people within a 3D virtual world: a whole online society called 'Second Life'. If you join this society you create an online character or personality – several if you like. Each character is called an 'avatar' and you can choose what your avatar looks like. For example, I might choose a male avatar, rather younger than my 'real' self and perhaps make him black. I might decide, unlike in my rather more sedate 'real' life, to go partying at nightclubs with young women (or at least female avatars) I meet in Second Life. This opens up all sorts of questions about gender and relationships and the possibilities open to us in doing gender within an everyday life that can include whole imagined worlds.

However, although Second Life may allow people to do their gender differently to the ways they do it in 'real' life, the virtual world still has its own rules and assumptions about gender and sexuality. Later in this chapter we will see that, in the real world, violence is a key problem in relationships between men and women. In Second Life there are strict rules about avoiding any abusive behaviour to others. The punishment for such behaviour is to be thrown out of the virtual world. Yet many of the rules and assumptions in Second Life take for granted some of our real-world notions. So although you do not have to be strictly human and could choose an avatar that is a cybergoth or a cartoonish bunny-like creature, even these avatars are usually assumed to be either male or female. And the bodies of the avatars seem to be always thin and young. In a world of supposedly endless possibilities, it is surprising how alike people's created characters look. Sociology can help understand why this might be so.

To begin to understand gender relations and relationships it is helpful to look historically at large-scale changes that can be characterized as a shift from a private patriarchy in which women's lives were controlled by the men in their family to a public patriarchy where there is greater freedom, but men still have considerable power within the workplace and the political sphere. However, private life has also changed, and intimate relationships arguably now involve more equality between women and men. A range of different ways of organizing intimate life have emerged, many of which may offer more control to women. The comparative section evaluates these alternative types of relationship and how they might be part of the reshaping of gender relations. Although positive changes have and continue to occur in how women and men relate, there are still major problems. In the final section of the chapter a critical eye is turned on one of these problems: violence. In looking at violence it is possible to see how the way society is organized constrains the way that individuals act and interact. Nevertheless there are still chances for individuals to exercise some agency, or control, over their actions.

A HISTORY OF GENDER RELATIONS(HIPS)

The strange brackets in the above subheading are meant to indicate that there are two levels at which women and men interact with each other: there are large-scale, more impersonal gender relations and intimate gendered relationships. At the large-scale level sociologists talk about the ways in which women as a social group compare to men as a social group. Concerns at that level are with general patterns in how the two groups are positioned in relation to each other within society. The usual framework employed to understand gender relations is the common sociological framework of social stratification and the associated inequalities. **Social stratification** refers to the different layers within society, the hierarchies organized around different groups. The major forms of stratification occur around class, ethnicity and, of course, gender. Women's social position has historically been, and many argue continues to be, one of disadvantage. Much research has been done on the extent to which there are gender inequalities so that women typically have worse jobs, get less pay, are likely to be poorer and more likely to be the victims of violence. As we will see, how gender relations operate at a large-scale level will impact on the way people conduct their intimate relationships.

From private to public patriarchy

Privacy and the space to develop a 'private' life are relatively recent luxuries and have meant different things for women than for men. The supposedly 'private' space of the family did not give anyone much room or time to themselves. For example, prior to modernity whole families commonly slept in one room. Well into the twentieth century children in many families, except the wealthiest, were expected to share a bed (Elias 2000/1939). While men might escape such cramped conditions, being allowed some leisure time to see friends or pursue their interests, women were usually expected to be constantly available to their families, even if they worked. Yet the very idea of having a life separate from or away from the 'public' is fairly new.

As Western society entered the modern era, the increasing complexity of society saw distinctions made between different parts of people's everyday lives. A key distinction was between those areas of life thought private and those thought public. 'Private' life was the realm where people conducted their family and other intimate relationships. It was an area supposedly governed by emotions and free from the harsh competitive struggle of the 'public' world of work and political life. The political sphere was where the public decision making central to maintaining an ordered society took place. Individuals were supposedly left to control their own 'private' life within the family and other intimate relationships. Nature rather than reason was what was thought to govern the bodily and emotional messiness of relationships. Women were thought closer to 'nature' and therefore suited to tasks within the 'private'. The messiness of women's bodies was supposed to make them incapable of the reason needed for 'proper' political debate and so they were actively excluded from public decision making; for example, they did not have the vote until the late nineteenth century or later. It was argued that their fathers and husbands were the ones who could better represent their political interests (Benhabib 1987; Pateman 1988). If women were to play a part in shaping their own destiny it was crucial that they gain access to these public decision-making processes and that is why the first-wave feminism of the nineteenth and early twentieth century (see Chapter 4) focused so much on the vote, with some attention to getting women access to other parts of the public sphere such as higher education and the workplace, especially the professions such as medicine and law.

There is some debate about how distinct the private and public areas of life are. Some have argued that the boundaries are rather blurred and shifting, and make sense only in relation to each other. So the private sphere does not describe an actual space but a category of things that are not public. And, conversely, the public sphere is a category containing things that are not domestic (Pateman 1988). These categories can be useful for explaining how gender relations have changed since the mid-twentieth century.

Western worlds before the late twentieth century were ones in which women's everyday lives were focused around family life, and their fathers and/or husbands had a lot of control over them. Sylvia Walby (1990, 1997) has called this **private patriarchy**. Patriarchy is a social system in which men as a group dominate women as a group. Walby suggests that there are six structures that make up patriarchy: paid work, household production, culture, sexuality, violence, and the state. These structures are linked, but their operation has changed in the shift away from private patriarchy. That was a system in which women were often financially dependent on men in their family, some not working at all or having to give up their work. In many of the better jobs, such as teaching, there were bans until the 1960s or 1970s against married women working. Those who did work typically earned poor wages and therefore were still reliant on having men to support them, especially for at least some period if they had children. Gradually, after the Second World War, all this began to change as more and more women started to go out to work and get more access to better jobs. Many women have achieved financial independence, and there have been changes that make divorce easier and provide some welfare to support lone mothers. This means that it is possible for women to live without having a man to support them. However, Walby (1990, 1997) argues that this does not mean that patriarchy disappears, but rather changes in form.

According to Walby (1990, 1997), gender relations now take the form of **public patriarchy**. Rather than women's everyday lives being under the control of individual men within their families, decisions affecting their lives are usually made by groups of men in the public world. Politicians, heads of big corporations, judges and other powerful groups are still overwhelmingly male. For example, in 2007, 417 of America's top 500 companies each had fewer than three women directors (Catalyst 2007). Many of the most powerful Western nations are fairly low down the rankings in terms of how many women are in parliament. A non-Western nation, Rwanda, does best as almost 50 per cent of those in its parliament are women. Germany is ranked 14th, with about 32 per cent of its decision makers being women. France is less impressive with around 19 per cent. In the UK, around 20 per cent of seats in parliament are occupied by women. The United States does quite poorly, having only about 16 per cent women among its representatives when the world average is about 17 per cent. Women make up only around 10 per cent of politicians elected in the Russian Federation (Inter-parliamentary Union 2007). This shows that, although women are no longer excluded from the public world, they have not achieved full equality. The new 'public' form of patriarchy does not exclude women from the public sphere, as private patriarchy did, but they are segregated into particular jobs and into the lower levels of the hierarchy. However, it is not simply a matter of public patriarchy having replaced private patriarchy.

Public patriarchy is now the dominant form within Western society, but private forms of patriarchy continue to exist. Older women who began their lives under the domestic system of patriarchy do not have the education, skills and work experience to find work that could make them independent, should they wish it. Within Britain certain ethnic groups, such as British Asians, tend to operate more on the private model and women in that group are more likely than white women to be largely dependent upon fathers and husbands. British Caribbean women are more tied to public patriarchy than are white women. Young women's lives are more likely to be affected by public patriarchy. This is because younger women are more likely to have an education and to get jobs that allow a degree of independence from individual men. This may change as they get older and start families, though this depends on whether and how they continue to work. Both types of patriarchy impact differently on different women depending on their class, age, position in the life course (for example, before or after having children) and ethnicity (Walby 1997).

Walby's explanation of how things have changed for women does recognize differences between women, but is centrally about Britain (with some discussion of the European Union). The broad outlines of her theory make reasonable sense of what has happened in other Western nations, although the details will differ: for example, African-American women may have moved further towards public patriarchy than whites in the United States. Latino-Americans are likely to occupy a similar position to British Asians. It is possible to extend Walby's analysis globally, in which case developing nations are likely to be characterized as ones in which women continue to be controlled via families. Yet this shows that there are limitations to her approach, because she tends to represent progress for women as a shift away from the constraints of private life.

Much common-sense thinking tends to portray 'private' life as an area where women have considerable status and control. Although sociologists might want to question the accuracy of common-sense ideas such as this (see below), they may want to recognize that women are not simply doormats. Walby is trying to think about how women have gained greater control over their own lives, but she focuses on how this has happened by them entering more into public life. Her vision of private life remains one of traditional male-breadwinner families. Others (Beck and Beck-Gernsheim 2002) agree that individualization processes have given women more freedom to live for themselves, rather than their families, but that this changes the character of private life as well. The private does not remain an unreconstructed realm in which women are inevitably under the thumb of men. Private life and families are also altered, and women have been active in bringing about these alterations by insisting that the personal is political.

The personal is political

The slogan 'the personal is political' exposed the artificiality of public/private distinctions. It highlighted that the work done in the public world relied upon women's toil in the home. The phrase was a demand to take notice of many of the issues crucial to most women's everyday lives but largely ignored by politicians and policy makers. It was a slogan that emerged from the second-wave feminist movement that was part of broad social revolutions in the 1960s and 1970s (see Chapter 4). Feminists began to examine all the aspects of women's experiences typically excluded from formal decision making. Sex, sexuality and violence were debated in political terms, as were other everyday issues such as the way people dressed and ate. Fundamentally, feminists examined intimate relationships between women and men as relationships of power.

Popular culture has tended to represent feminists as man-haters and lesbians – the implication is that being a lesbian is a terrible thing. These portrayals are a reaction to the challenge feminists made to the existing social order, including to cosy ideas about relationships being just about love. They emphasized the political nature of relationships with men but also examined the way women related to each other.

It is true that feminists were critical of men and many were quite blunt, accepting that their view might be controversial. However, most feminists concentrated on criticizing the patriarchal system. Men had an advantage over women because they had better access to the resources society had to offer. Thus men were able to exercise power over women, both at a large-scale and a personal level. Intimate relationships between the sexes were therefore always power relationships (Millett 1972/1970). Individual men making changes would help, but this would not bring liberation for women unless the way society operated changed.

At the beginning of the feminist movement in the late 1960s and early 1970s, some feminist groups or events included men (Whelehan 1995: 177), but feminists became frustrated by men's tendency to monopolize meetings or groups and found more could be achieved without them (Phillips 1991: 98). Some men continued to provide support for the feminist movement, but did so by forming their own groups to examine how they might relate to women in better ways (Messner 1997) and/or providing background support such as childcare at feminist conferences.

Feminist conferences demonstrated how all aspects of women's everyday relationships with men came under political examination. Even things such as the way houses and furniture were arranged were up for criticism. At a feminist gathering in New Zealand in 1979 there was an architect who 'presented house plans that would alleviate the oppression of household duties' and 'another group re-arranged the three piece suite to get rid of male oppression' (McShane 1979: 7–8). Now this may seem laughable at one level (and certainly makes me laugh), but at another level it can be seen as a quite radical rethink of everyday ways of doing things that we take for granted. Prior to the 1980s most women were expected to focus their energies on work within the home, and that work was usually repetitive and isolating, and prevented women doing other things (see Oakley 1974). Rearranging the home might be part of rethinking how heterosexual couples relate. And the three-piece suite is one example of how everyday objects might reinforce ideas about men as the head of the household. Besides the sofa there might be a large 'dad's chair' given prime position in the living room and a smaller 'mum's chair' in the corner, reflecting traditional ideas about the proper role of women as self-sacrificing and devoted to making men comfortable. These are rather flippant examples among what were serious attempts to think critically about relationships between women and men as relationships of power.

By the 1980s feminist debates about sexuality and relationships erupted into what have become known (at least in North America) as the 'sex wars' (Duggan and Hunter 2006). The two opposing camps in this 'war' were the anti-pornography feminists such as Andrea Dworkin (1981) and the anti-censorship feminists such as Carol Vance (1984). The two perspectives can also be characterized as opposing a view of (heterosexual) sex and sexuality as dangerous for women to a view of the importance for women of finding pleasure in some form(s) of sexual expression. The anti-pornography camp saw pornography as degrading to women and as fundamental in creating a culture in which women were expected to be sexually available to men and encountered violence if they were not. This group was committed to achieving legal restrictions on pornography; in other words, it wanted more censorship. Those feminists who opposed this group challenged the view of sexuality as inherently negative and were against censorship, primarily because they argued that it would be used to suppress expressions of alternative sexualities, especially gay and lesbian sexualities. Anti-censorship feminists challenged heterosexism.

A crucial part of analysing the political nature of relationships was the development of the concept of heterosexism (see Evans 1995: 16; Jackson and Scott 1996: 12–17). **Heterosexism** refers to the way that heterosexuality is presented as 'natural' and homosexuality seen as deviant. Just as sexism describes prejudices against members of the sex thought inferior (women), heterosexism describes prejudices against those whose sexual orientation does not fit with what is thought normal and 'natural'. Heterosexism existed within feminist movements as well as outside them. Heterosexual feminists were not always sympathetic towards their lesbian sisters, often because some felt that lesbians were saying that all feminists must adopt lesbian relationships. How could women improve their social position if they were 'sleeping with the enemy'? Some feminists argued that women needed to expend their energy on building positive relationships with other women, separately from men if possible.

Separatism was much misunderstood. Most lesbian feminists did see sexuality as central to women's oppression (as women's social position was termed by them). Who you related to and how was not just a personal matter of your 'nature', but something you could and should make choices and decisions about. Some lesbian feminists did argue that women should withdraw their sexual attention from men and focus it on women. However, very few lesbian feminists took a radically separatist position, as most realized it was neither really practical nor even desirable to live completely cut off from men. Some lesbians had sons and most had close relationships with some men, be they brothers, fathers or male homosexual friends. Nevertheless, it was important that they challenged heterosexism by saying and showing that relationships between women, whether sexual or not, could be fulfilling and rewarding, and did not have to be secondary to a relationship with a man (Holmes 2000b).

Of course, not all men have power over all women, and relationships between women are not inevitably without problems or free from power struggles. Feminists found that they could not assume that all women had the same experiences and the same priorities. There were conflicts within the feminist movement, but that was an important part of coming to a better understanding of women in all their diversity. Equally, how much control particular men have over their lives and the women in them varies considerably. Dorothy Smith and R.W. Connell are just two sociologists who have done a great deal of work on gender as a relation. Smith (e.g. 1987) has argued that gender is a fundamental part of relations of ruling within a capitalist society. The very ways in which men's dominant social position is maintained rely on organizing and thinking about men as rational actors in the big wide world of the market and women as daily engaging with particular emotional relationships within a small, local, family-based sphere.

Smith endeavours to rethink sociology so that it can better take account of the everyday lives of women. Connell's (e.g. 1995, 2005) analysis is similar, but also illustrates the variety of forms masculinity can take. The extent to which women are shaped and constrained, and men shaped and enabled, within their everyday lives varies according to a complex blend of class, ethnic background, age, level of education and other factors. Power operates in all relationships, but what feminists were identifying was the particular ways in which relationships between women and men were lived out within a patriarchal system that *tends* to constrain women and benefit men. However, feminists and their male supporters were also suggesting that this could be changed, and that new and more equal ways of relating could be found.

COMPARISONS: CONVENTIONAL AND NON-CONVENTIONAL RELATIONSHIPS

Young Westerners are highly likely to have experienced divorce within their everyday lives. In North America, Europe and Australasia around one in every two marriages now ends in divorce. For second and third marriages the odds of success are even worse. Cohabitation may be increasingly popular, but it is often a prelude to marriage and is not necessarily long lasting (Office of National Statistics 2002; Kiernan 2004).

Traditional relationships are changing, and arguably the long-term coupling of 'till death do us part' is being replaced by 'pure relationships' in which people stay together only as long as they find satisfaction in the relationship (Giddens 1992). Giddens claims that such new types of relationship have many positive aspects; for example, they are more flexible and more equal. Instead of people basing their relationships on fairly static roles where men were expected to be the powerful providers and women the compliant nurturers, people now have to negotiate the terms of their relationship. Who will do what around the house, will they have sex with other people? Giddens thinks that these new, more democratic, forms of intimacy will also positively influence other parts of society. This optimism seems to be based on the idea that if men learn to act more fairly by debating with their intimate partners then they will take the lessons learned out into their workplace and the wider world. It is a nice idea, but not well supported by evidence about what happens in people's everyday intimate lives.

Intimate life, despite important changes, continues to be a realm in which both the physical and emotional work of maintaining relationships is divided by gender. There really is no gentle way to say it: men do very little of this work. Obviously there are exceptions. I am mindful that, as I sit writing this, my male partner brings me toast, and that I never vacuum. Nevertheless, there have been numerous studies of how housework is divided up between heterosexual couples and even including household maintenance, lawnmowing and the like, most women do a lot more housework. The gap has closed a little, many argue because women are doing less, but most studies suggest that *typically* women still do about twice as many hours of housework as men (e.g. Baxter 2005; Sullivan 2006; Boje 2007). Fighting over the washing-up is not just about personal standards of cleanliness, but is a gendered struggle to establish who is responsible for the household work. If you ever hear men say 'Can I *help* you with the washing-up?' to their womenfolk it is interesting to ponder how this implies that it is *really* a woman's job. Even where women work full-time and earn more than their husbands they are still likely to do the greater proportion of the housework. Women usually find their load gets even heavier once children are born and they find they are made ultimately responsible for childcare (Hochschild 1989; Gjerdingen and Center 2005; Sullivan 2006).

Similarly, responsibility for emotional sharing is still highly gendered (Erickson 2005). Giddens (1992) has argued that disclosing personal details about yourself to someone is crucial in forming and maintaining intimacy. In particular it is felt that the disclosure of feelings is extremely important, especially to women

(Brannen and Collard 1982; Duncombe and Marsden 1993, 1995). There is some evidence that when men do disclose they tend to disclose about their political views and things of which they are proud. Women meanwhile tend, it seems, to disclose their fears and their feelings – especially about their parents (Peplau 1994: 26). I suspect that the type of things disclosed may be highly culturally specific, with possibly significant differences even among the relatively similar cultures of North America (Peplau's study was in Boston) and Britain. However, men's seemingly greater reluctance to talk about feelings seems to be common, at least in the English-speaking West (Duncombe and Marsden 1993, 1995; Peplau 1994: 25–26).

But disclosing intimacy is not the only type of talk that is important, nor the only marker of love. Doing things for each other and even small physical shows of affection can all be part of a caring that is central in entangling people within intimacy. Cancian (1986) has argued that these ways of showing love have been undervalued because of the dominance of feminine styles of loving that privilege verbally disclosing feelings. Styles of intimacy may be gendered, and it may be that men learn or take on ways of feeling that are more about touching than talking.

Relationships that are different from traditional ones may be one way to try to achieve more equality. Non-heterosexual relations, friendships and living apart are just some examples. For example, social changes affecting male homosexual and lesbian relationships led many non-heterosexuals to form 'families of choice' (Weston 1991). New stories about their relationships emerge, in which those friends and lovers closest to them are referred to as 'family'. Even if they might be critical of traditional family values and ways of living, non-heterosexuals use the term family in ways that show their wish for belonging and forms of care associated with that term. As old ties break down, and especially for those excluded from previous notions of 'family', people creatively invent ties. Social changes do not simply destroy 'the family' and other relationships, rather people find new ways to relate (Weeks *et al.* 2001). Some of these might have advantages over traditional relationships. The new forms may involve more equal divisions of labour and allow partners more freedom in what they do and how they relate than the traditional roles of husband and wife. Friendship may be becoming the favoured model for 'good' relationships.

For many people the line between family and friends is becoming blurred. The kind of help and support usually offered to people by their kin is now often provided by close friends. And many people also now have relationships with kin that are more like friendships; for example, going clothes shopping or on nights out with their mum (Pahl and Spencer 2004). Some people take this further and rely centrally on friends in creating an intimate life. Roseneil and Budgeon (2004), for example, tell the story of Karen and Polly, two heterosexual women who are good friends and each have children. Partly because of failed relationships with men, they decide to buy a house together and commit to bringing up their children together. They do not have a sexual relationship with each other, and sometimes have boyfriends, but they do not let this interfere with their arrangement to join forces to try to provide a stable, loving environment for their children to grow in. Another example is couples who do not live together, either because of their work or because they do not want to fall into traditional patterns like fighting over who does the dishes. There are couples who live apart together (LATs) by keeping separate houses near to each other, and other couples who live some way apart and travel to see each other when they can. For women this might be a way to avoid taking on the role of the traditional wife, doing all the cooking, cleaning and caring. Women in LAT and distance relationships, do seem to find that they feel more independent and have some freedom from emotion work (Holmes 2004; Levin 2004). For most couples who do cohabit there are continual struggles over who does the work, but in some relationships there are also problems with violence.

THINKING CRITICALLY: THE PROBLEM OF VIOLENCE

Violence against women

Within everyday life violence plays a part in how gender is produced as a relation to others. The kinds of violence that women endure are likely to be different to the kinds that men experience. Men are more likely to experience random violence from strangers out in the streets. These kinds of violence are linked to expectations that they use violence to prove their masculinity, although many may resist this (Connell 1995). Women, on the other hand, are typically violently assaulted by people that they know. For instance, Unifem: the United Nations Development Fund for Women (2007) estimates that worldwide about half of women murder victims are killed by current or former husbands or partners. At a conservative estimate, around one-quarter of women have experienced physical or sexual abuse from partners or ex-partners. As many as one in five women are likely to have survived attempted rape or rape. These are sobering statistics on the extent of **sexual violence**, which is defined as physical, verbal, visual or sexual acts directed against women *as women* (Kelly 1997). Liz Kelly (1997) argues that there is a continuum of sexual violence, all the way from small acts like wolf whistling up to violent rape. In addition, there are other types of violence that have gendered aspects, such as criminal violence, medical violence (such as cosmetic surgery) and visual violence like that in movies. However, the focus on sexual violence is considered crucial because it shows how violence is a crucial tool used to control women.

The kinds of violence women experience are related to being a woman. Anti-pornography feminists have argued that common-sense ideas about women as sex objects who should be on display and available for male pleasure, cause violence against women (e.g. Dworkin 1981). Feminists against censorship (see Vance 1984) disagree, pointing out that pornography is not always violent and whether it causes violence against women depends on other factors such as a particular culture's tolerance of violence generally. For example, where corporal punishment is used in schools, or the death penalty still exists, such societies tend to have higher levels of violent crime, including sexually violent crime. These are just some of the attempts to explain what produces different experiences of violence for women to those of men.

Sociologists explain violence as resulting from social factors. This is an alternative to one of the most unhelpful ways of thinking about violence, which assumes that men are naturally violent and women are naturally non-violent. This does not explain how it is that not all men are violent and some women are. And, if it is 'natural', how can it change? Instead sociologists explore how the way society is organized (into social institutions) and the way we think and talk (discourses) affect the levels and types of violence that occur and which groups are most affected. R.W. Connell (1995, 2002) has suggested that social institutions such as families, the education system and the workplace are masculinized to promote male violence. The emphasis put on boys' achievements in contact sports at school is just one example of the way violence is encouraged. Anthony Giddens (1992) argues that there has been an increase in male violence against women since the late twentieth century, as men have felt threatened by women's greater equality and sexual liberation. However, it may be that violence has not especially increased, it is just that more violence is being reported. The point is that violence is a part of many intimate relationships.

Domestic or family violence

A classic sociological study of violence against wives (Dobash and Dobash 1979) provided some insight into 'domestic violence'. Now this is usually known as 'family violence', it includes more types of violence but tends to obscure the fact that women are much more likely to be harmed (Nazroo 1999). Dobash and

Dobash acknowledge that women are usually the victims of violence within relationships, and argue that this is the case because we live in a patriarchal society that has traditionally allowed men to treat women as their property. Husbands' rights to beat their wives have been legally supported in the past, or at least seldom punished. Various court cases in Western nations confirmed that men could use force on their wives, as long as they did not overdo it. Also the law has previously enshrined men's right of sexual access to their wives whenever they please. In the nineteenth century married women had no legal existence as individuals; their husbands controlled all their property and were deemed responsible for their wives. And, as far as the justice system in these nations was concerned, a man could not be charged with raping his wife. When she said 'I do' at the altar she was deemed to have made herself sexually available to her husband whenever he might wish. It was not until the late 1980s or 1990s that many Western nations introduced laws against rape within marriage. Thus, women have traditionally been in a vulnerable position within marriage (Brook 2007). However, many people find it difficult to understand why women do not just leave violent husbands.

Dobash and Dobash (1979) offered explanations of why women often remain with violent husbands (and this can extend to de facto partners), which have been confirmed and added to by later research (e.g. Cavanagh *et al.* 2001). The first point to make is that some women do leave violent partners, but some return. It is not surprising that some return if we recall that a large proportion of women murder victims are killed by former husbands/ partners. One of the threats violent male partners use is that they will harm or kill their wife/partner if she leaves. And if women stay they often do so in the belief that things will change, or that it is their responsibility to make the relationship work. Their partners are often very apologetic after violent incidents and promise to change.

Even if there comes a point at which women may cease to believe things will change they may lack resources or feasible alternatives. They may be economically dependent on their partner, or have nowhere to stay. Although women's refuges do exist, which will offer safe temporary accommodation for battered women and their children, the demand for refuge considerably exceeds the places available. For example, in Scotland in 2002–2003, almost 4,000 women and children were admitted to refuges but around the same number had to be turned away (Scottish Women's Aid 2007). Similarly, in the same period in Australia, only around one in two of the women requesting accommodation on an average day could be accommodated (Australian Institute of Health and Welfare 2005: 8). If women do not have family who can or wish to help, there may be nowhere for them and any children to go.

Even if they do have somewhere to go, many women fear that partners will pursue them and harm them or their children even more. This fear is not unrealistic and women are aware that there is likely to be little to effectively protect them. Policing of domestic violence has improved considerably, but things such as restraining orders do not ensure women's safety. This is demonstrated by the high incidence of ex-partners among female homicide perpetrators.

Finally, women may find it difficult to leave their violent husbands because there is a degree of social acceptance of violence against women. This may be less than was previously the case, due to zero tolerance campaigns (for example, 'To violence against women, Australia says no'). Nevertheless, there are still misconceptions that women must have done something to deserve being beaten, as though violence is ever acceptable. Of course, there is also the question of whether women are sometimes violent to their male partners.

Violent women

Various studies suggest that women's violence to their husbands is fairly extensive. Conflict is part of most relationships and may involve various degrees of physical fighting. However, most people would agree that there is a big difference between the occasional competitive arm wrestle to decide who has to do the dishes and continued punches to the face leaving a black eye. As Nazroo (1999) has argued, most of the studies showing women as highly violent to partners collected data in ways that neglected such differences in the degree of violence. He suggested that the types of violence in which women engaged were far more likely to be small, occasional uses of physical force such as slapping or kicking. While much of this violence may have malicious motives it usually inflicts little damage on partners. The type of violence to which many women are subject from their partners is far more likely to see them hospitalized with often serious injuries such as broken bones. And if women do sometimes inflict more physical harm upon a partner, Nazroo notes that it is often in response to years of battering. However, women do sometimes instigate violence.

Women may inflict violence upon their children (or elders under their care), which tends to challenge cultural notions of women as naturally, benignly maternal and caring. With children there are varying degrees of violence used, and the point at which 'discipline' becomes abuse is highly contested. Often the contests occur across cultural and class boundaries. For example, white middle-class European-derived cultures have developed ideas about child rearing that frown on smacking. Such people form the dominant groups and hold political power in many Western nations and are therefore able to impose their distaste for physically punishing children onto others. Thus laws against smacking children have been introduced in much of Scandinavia and in New Zealand, and have been proposed in Britain (Nicholson 2008). This then criminalizes those with more physical approaches to child discipline. It ignores the fact that middle-class parents may have considerably more material and emotional resources to help them to deal with children without resorting to violence. They can afford babysitters or summer camps to give them a break. They are likely to live in safer areas or have gardens where kids can play outside unsupervised. Middle-class white mothers are likely to have more control over their work, more leisure time and fewer financial worries than working-class and non-white mothers. They are likely to be able to afford help with care for elderly relatives. Living up to ideals of smiling, patient motherhood is liable to be difficult when you constantly work overtime, you haven't had a holiday in years, are looking after a fragile old parent and the rent is overdue. Various class and cultural groups may also disagree about ideals of mothering (Arendell 2000). It may be that hitting children is seen as a legitimate and necessary part of child rearing. Again the degree of violence used is crucial, and anything that inflicts lasting bruises or more serious injuries on children is likely to be seen as unacceptable in all communities.

While material deprivation and accompanying emotional weariness may contribute to child (and elder) abuse, this does not mean that such abuse is inevitably more widespread among disadvantaged women. What it means is that those women are often likely to be under a much higher degree of monitoring, partly because they are highly likely to have to rely on some social welfare. For those who are wealthy and privileged it is much easier to hide any violence that may be occurring when they are very unlikely to have to submit to any assessment by welfare agencies and have considerable control over their privacy. But also many women in highly restricting and deprived situations do help create a loving and largely non-violent home environment.

Changing violent gender relations

Social factors such as economic situation and cultural learning have a great deal of impact on when and how violence enters gender relations and relations with children; but women are not just passive victims of patriarchy. They may on occasion fight back, and they may visit violence upon children. But women may also find ways to take control of their lives without resorting to harmful forms of violence. These might include some of the non-conventional experiments in intimacy mentioned above. They might include bringing up children on their own. People can make choices, but they do so within the constraints of the social situation.

Creating gender relations and relationships free from harmful violence requires not just individual but social changes. Yes it will help if individual men can recognize and address their violent behaviour. Certainly it is good if women do everything they can to protect themselves. However, these individual efforts remain difficult and frail unless there are changes in the wider social system. Where violence is glorified through school, sports, the military and the media as crucial to the expression of masculinity, it is difficult for men to be non-violent. Where women are financially dependent on men it is difficult for them to escape violence. When a society punishes schoolchildren with caning or its criminals by putting them to death, then the message is that violence is the way to make people conform to social rules. This can mean that women and men who attempt to alter the rules around gender are thought to deserve punishment. Relating more respectfully is possible. To move towards more respectful and equal relations involves conflict around how women and men *should* relate within general social hierarchies and within intimate relations. Conflict sometimes is violent as people react to new or alternative gender relations that threaten their beliefs or their privilege or their desire to control. There are steps forward and steps back. If we can challenge ideas that men are naturally aggressive and women naturally caring, then it becomes much easier to allow that how women and men relate to each other can be changed. If gender relations are socially constructed, then it is reasonable to expect that they can be constructed differently. How relations between women and men should be constructed is hugely contested. At a very basic level there is widespread social acceptance that women and men *should* be equal and that relations that are violently harmful are unacceptable. Struggling towards more equitable and respectful gender relations is staggeringly important in making everyday life not just bearable but loveable.

SUMMARY

Gender permeates our everyday relationships, even though we are not always aware of it. How gender operates has certainly changed at a societal level as women have gained rights and entered the workforce in greater numbers. This has made many women less dependent on individual men for their survival, but the overall social system remains one in which men continue to have control. Although women's greater independence may allow them to have more choice about who and how they love, intimate relationships remain heavily gendered. The way in which gender inequalities operate within intimate life was shown by comparing different types of relationship, from conventional married couples to lesbian couples to couples who choose not to live together. Violence might erupt in some couples, and it is more often women who are harmed. This is not an inevitable outcome to be explained as a result of men's supposedly violent natures. Some women are violent and not all men are. Couples typically engage in struggles over who does the dishes, over who says 'I love you', and how they care for each other physically and emotionally. It is possible that some less conventional relationships have more gender equality. However, despite much progress, our social world still contains hurdles for women in achieving control over their lives both at the private and public levels. This does not mean that all men are in control and all women are downtrodden victims. What it demonstrates is that gender is a relation to others, but a hierarchical relation that is open to struggle and to change. While there are social structures and social norms that constrain people in gendered ways, there are always possibilities for resistance, as the next chapter shows.

4

RESISTING GENDER
IN EVERYDAY LIFE

INTRODUCTION

Nothing annoyed me more as a child than being told: 'Girls can't do that.' Usually this made me more determined to do whatever 'that' was. This did not make me especially rebellious, but in small ways I resisted gender norms. I climbed trees, I played soccer instead of netball. And I am not the only one who has tried to cross the lines between the pink and blue worlds. Every year students tell me stories of little boys they know who like to play dress-up with make-up and skirts, or girls who love trucks and will not go near pink. And then there are the grown-ups. British comedian Eddy Izzard, for example, refers to himself as an 'executive transvestite'. Unlike drag queens, who imitate more conventional feminine styles, Izzard usually wears trouser suits, but with materials, colours and/or or styling that are usually thought 'feminine'. He dons lipstick and eye shadow. His doing of gender is rather ambiguous. These everyday actions are some of the ways in which gender is resisted.

Resistance is the struggle against injustice and the fight for control over one's own life and actions. The history of this struggle is a long one for women, with more organized forms of resistance emerging in the nineteenth century. This chapter examines these feminist movements and compares them to forms of politics organized around masculinity. This enables a comparative exploration of how and why gendered resistance operates differently depending on the position of different groups of women and men in relation to hierarchies of power. However, if it is the case that society has become subject to processes of individualization, have new, more personalized forms of resistance become common? We critically examine some of the current everyday ways in which people might try to resist gender norms. Everything from fashion to films to face cream can illustrate how some individuals attempt to do gender differently and to bring wider changes in gender norms. Throughout, there will be considerations of how successful these various efforts at resistance are.

HISTORIES OF RESISTANCE

In the fifteenth century a woman called Christine de Pisan wrote a book called *The City of Ladies*, which sets out to refute 'all manner of philosophers, poets and orators too numerous to mention, who all seem to speak with one voice and are unanimous in their view that female nature is wholly given up to vice' (Pisan 2005: 2). She was annoyed with the constant slandering of women that many of the scholars she read engaged in, and set out to examine and argue against the claims they made. For example, in warning men about the dangers of corrupt women, some learned men encouraged their fellows to avoid all women as abominations. Pisan's (2005: 9) retort was that this was a faulty argument akin to saying that fire should be avoided because one person burnt himself. In reply to claims that women are weak, naturally ignorant and unfit for education and for governing, Pisan tells of women throughout history who have shown strength, intelligence and good judgement. She points out that it is lack of education that limits women's powers of reasoning, not natural incapacity. She also dismisses those, sadly enduring, claims that women really want to be raped, even if they say no. On this and many other points, she resists much of the common 'wisdom' of her time about women. She carefully establishes that 'women are more than capable of undertaking any task which requires physical strength or of learning any discipline which requires discernment and intelligence' (Pisan 2005: 60). Thus she challenges ideas that sought to justify women's inferior social position as 'naturally' ordained.

Two centuries after Pisan, another famous piece of writing appeared protesting against woman's lowly social status. In *A Vindication of the Rights of Woman*, Mary Wollstonecraft (mother to Mary Shelley, who wrote *Frankenstein*) carefully applied new liberal ideas about individual rights to women. Her argument was that women should be recognized as the intellectual and social equals of men. They should have access to the same education and opportunities as men. In order for this to take place, the dominant ideas of her time needed to be challenged. Women were thought inferior to men and incapable of reason. However, Wollstonecraft was adamant that women were capable of reason, and that any shortcomings in understanding they may have were a result of their lack of education. With education women would be able to think for themselves and ultimately fend for themselves. Women, she argued, had the right to be independent and to exercise some control over their lives (Wollstonecraft 1985/1792). These liberal ideas about equality between women and men have become dominant in the Western world, and individuals or groups who disagree tend to be marginal. However, in the eighteenth century Wollstonecraft's suggestion that women should be treated as independent, intelligent individuals was radical. She was resisting much of the learned opinion and common-sense thinking of her era. Just one of many examples is Dr Johnson's 'witticism' in the eighteenth century, when asked what he thought of women preachers. He replied: 'Sir, a woman's preaching is like a dog's walking on his hind legs. It is not done well, but you are surprised to find it done at all' (see Woolf 1929: 95).

Christine de Pisan and Mary Wollstonecraft were privileged women, who were able to devote their time to learning and to writing and refuting such 'wisdom' as Dr Johnson's. Not many women have had such luxury, as Virginia Woolf (1929: 4) notes in her famous essay *A Room of One's Own*, where she argues that 'a woman must have money and a room of her own if she is to write'. In other words, in order to have intellectual freedom and the leisure to use it to write, a certain level of economic independence is required.

Thus the ability for most women to resist norms and conventions and dictates about femininity have been limited given their historical reliance on men for survival. However, more mass forms of resistance emerged, partly as a result of the economic changes accompanying industrialization, which gradually created some opportunities for women to survive economically outside of a patriarchal family. At the very least more women might have some money of their own, which they could use to pursue their own interests. These interests might be political, and indeed as industrialization took off in Europe in the mid-eighteenth century a mass movement began to emerge demanding rights for women.

First-wave feminism

The nineteenth-century swell of women demanding 'emancipation', or greater freedom for women, concentrated mainly on the vote and on women's entry to education and the professions. In retrospect, this upsurge of activity around women's rights was referred to as first-wave feminism. The word feminism to describe such political activity on behalf of women did not come into usage until the 1890s. Prior to that date the various debates and activities involved were referred to as 'the woman question'. This 'question' was about what women's position should be in modern society. The notion that 'a woman's place is in the home' was being challenged, at least for middle-class women who were not already working outside the home as their working-class sisters were (Rendall 1985).

There was some attention to issues affecting working-class women, such as the problems of long working hours and poor conditions, and some working-class women activists were involved in suffrage movements, but these were often issues taken up within class politics. Men's dominance of the unions central to that class politics sometimes saw the position of women workers worsened (for example, the hours they could work limited by legislation supposedly designed to protect them) rather than improved as men fought to compete with women workers who were cheaper to hire (Hartmann 1981). Other marginalized groups of women were addressed to some degree. For example, there was a long struggle against state regulation of prostitution, fronted by British feminist Josephine Butler but international in scope. In Britain this centred around trying to get rid of the Contagious Diseases Act, which could be used to lock poor women in special hospitals just on suspicion of prostitution. The aim was to protect men, especially the military, from the spread of venereal and other sexually transmitted diseases. It is telling, however, that women were targeted, rather than criminalizing the male clients of prostitutes. After 16 years of trying, the laws were eventually overturned (Jordan 2001). This was one of a number of successes, but the first wave tended to be dominated by middle-class women and their issues.

The advances made by Victorian women were largely ones of interest to middle-class women previously sequestered at home. The feminism of the time was heavily based on liberalism, as extended to include women by Mary Wollstonecraft. The focus was thus on education and on the opportunities for individuals to live up to their potential (Whelehan 1995: 27–34). And opportunities for middle-class women did indeed expand. Universities became open to women in most Western nations in the second half of the nineteenth century, and women graduates started to emerge. During this period professions such as the law and medicine became open to women, and women doctors and lawyers began to appear. Late that century, nation states – first, New Zealand in 1893 – began to grant women the right to vote in elections (Evans 1977). Women were gaining the ability to be independent.

A different kind of woman was emerging; she was dubbed 'the New Woman', who as well as enjoying some economic independence was throwing off some of the everyday constraints attached to being a Victorian woman. There were movements to ban corseting, which often damaged women's bodies and in rare cases led to death. Dress reform movements sprang up in the latter part of the century, proposing that women wear more 'rational' clothing. Knickerbockers were adopted by some of the women in this group – one woman even wore them to her wedding. Often dress reform was tied to practical issues such as needing more appropriate clothing to ride the newly invented bicycle. Cycling clubs were very popular across the British Empire, especially among young women. The bodily freedom of movement cycling gave was often a new and valued experience, which made women think about challenging other restrictions (Holmes 1991).

First-wave feminists sometimes used their bodies as instruments of resistance, to protest against both large-scale and more everyday gender constraints. For example, as the campaign for female suffrage (votes for women) developed a radical wing in early twentieth-century Britain, some suffragettes chained themselves to railings at the Houses of Parliament to symbolize their lack of political freedom. When arrested for these and other activities they would also go on hunger strikes to draw attention to their cause (Green 1997). There was also an incident that could have been, but was not, what we now call a suicide attack. A feminist called Emily Davison walked out in front of the King's horse at the Epsom Derby in 1913, carrying the banner of the Women's Social and Political Union, a suffrage organization. She was trampled to death by the horse (Stanley and Morley 1988). Thus there were connections made between the freedom of individual bodies and wider social freedoms. However, attentions to 'personal' freedom were arguably less central to first-wave feminism than they were in the second wave.

Second-wave feminism

One of the key features of second-wave feminism across Western nations was a focus on the idea that 'the personal is political', and this changed notions of what and how to resist. As discussed in Chapter 3, modern Western societies have centred around distinctions between the public and private spheres of life. Politics has traditionally been the arena in which matters of the public or common good have been debated and decided. The private sphere has been characterized largely in domestic terms, as a sanctuary from the cares of the world and a space in which people may decide freely about 'personal' matters such as love, sex, child rearing, and so on. Of course this is not necessarily the reality, these are ideals. However, this distinction has had a great deal of force in determining what gets onto the political agenda. Things pertaining to the private sphere have been excluded from political debate and supposedly left to 'personal' decision making. Second-wave feminists drew attention to the fact that many of the issues thus ignored were crucial to women's everyday existence. In Chapter 3, I discussed how feminists subjected intimate relationships to political scrutiny. Other key issues that challenged the private/public distinction were a woman's right to control her own body, and the need for childcare (Seidman 1994; Holmes 2007b: 114–116).

A defining issue for second-wave feminism was the insistence on 'a woman's right to choose' if and when to have children. Most women's lives in the twentieth century still revolved around motherhood. The arrival of the contraceptive pill in the 1960s made it possible for more women to take greater control of their reproductive capacities without having to rely on the assistance of men. However, the pill was usually available only to married women, and feminists noted that there was still far from decent access for most women to safe and effective contraception. In that case, they argued, access to safe abortion must be provided so that women did not have to have unwanted children (Holmes 2007b: 115–116).

Having children may ideally be a joy, but lack of access to alternative childcare makes mothering difficult. Despite entering the workforce in increasing numbers since the mid-twentieth century women have retained the major responsibility for child rearing. Many men may be more involved as fathers but it is still largely women who make career and other sacrifices to care for children. Family childcare, especially from a woman's mother, has become less available, with extended families often geographically distant and grandmothers highly likely to be working. Meanwhile, there continues to be a shortage of childcare available in many Western nations, even if women can afford it. This has huge implications for women's ability to succeed, or even compete, within the workforce (Hochschild 1989; Hochschild and Ehrenreich 2004; Pocock 2006).

While choices for women have expanded since the nineteenth century, this has mainly taken the form of women gaining access to the world of work, while still trying to provide care for families. Trying to juggle work and family life is a major difficulty for many women (Hochschild 1989; Pocock 2006). Interestingly enough, in this century fertility rates have dropped below replacement level in most Western nations and this trend is starting to spread to developing countries (Morgan and Taylor 2006). One wonders whether, consciously or unconsciously, many women are going on strike. They are perhaps withholding their reproductive labour in protest at the conditions under which they are expected to mother. This may be a crucial form of resistance in the twenty-first century.

So far in discussing resistance I have focused mostly on women, which makes sense given that it is marginal groups that need to resist a social system in which they are disadvantaged. However, if gender is a relation then what men do is important in how that resistance operates. Whether women's resistance is successful can depend on how men, both those in power and those individually close to women, respond to it. Also if there is to be change in gender relations then there need to be challenges made to how masculinity is 'done'. But this is a rather different enterprise to women's resistance to a system that disadvantages them, and can therefore serve as a good comparison to help further understand gender resistance.

COMPARING RESISTANCE: RESISTING MASCULINITY

Largely as a response to women's challenges to male dominance, men have mounted both personal and collective efforts to reconfirm or to rethink their masculinity. However, gender resistance takes different forms for men because the social system is one that typically benefits men more than women. Men are still likely to be paid more than women, more likely to be in high-status jobs and positions of power and to do less of the undervalued domestic work including caring for children and the elderly (Holmes 2007b: 6–11). Men enjoy the privileges of a patriarchal society, even if they are critical of it, so it is not surprising that many men are not very interested in changing things. However, some men are involved in challenging male privilege and not all men are equally privileged.

Unlike feminist tendencies to consider which groups of women were most oppressed, a lot of masculinity politics focuses around which men are most privileged. Whether the most privileged form of masculinity is referred to as 'hegemonic masculinity' (Connell 1995) or 'classic masculinity' (Morgan 1993), or 'the masculine ideal' (Segal 1990), we can summarize its key aspects. Adhering to this form of masculinity involves having a physically powerful and well-controlled body, a stoic and non-emotional approach to life and, related to that, pursuing power and success in an organized and even ruthless manner. Rejection of the feminine and the homosexual as utterly opposite to 'real' manliness is also typically central in displaying hegemonic masculinity. This supposedly supreme maleness is active, rational and in charge. Defending this dominant form of masculinity is in itself a form of politics, and men with political power often reinforce the privilege of men like themselves (Connell 1995).

As with femininity, dominant versions of masculinity are fundamentally middle class, white and Western. Michael Kimmel (2005: 415) says that the global version of this kind of manliness is easy to identify:

> You can see him sitting in first-class waiting rooms in airports, or in elegant business hotels the world over, wearing a designer business suit, speaking English, eating 'continental' cuisine, talking on his cell phone, his laptop computer plugged into any electrical outlet, while he watches CNN International on television.

As Morgan (1993) notes, this classical, rational, controlled masculinity is usually differentiated from a grotesque form of masculinity associated with working-class men. Grotesque masculinity describes the way in which working-class men are devalued within society. Their bodies are often represented as excessive (often obese) – think Homer Simpson. However, there are more aesthetic representations of male working-class bodies, which are sometimes sexualized as the object of middle-class women's desires. This was evident in a Coca-Cola advertisement some years ago where women office workers eagerly awaited their 'Diet Coke break', when they would go to their office window to watch a well-toned young construction worker nearby strip off his shirt and drink a Coke. Such representations associate working-class masculinity with nature and a potential for violence, signalled by muscles. However, grotesque masculinity is usually disdained by the middle classes. Within the working class, it is celebrated. This could be understood as a form of resistance to dominant forms of masculinity, but it is often a very destructive form of resistance involving fast cars, drinking, fighting and dying young (Connell 1995).

Non-white and non-Western masculinities are also marginalized and the effects of this are being played out on the local and the global stage. Within many nations the debilitating effects of histories of slavery and colonization have left many black men subject to lives of poverty, un- or under-employment, violence and, for some, incarceration. Everywhere men's everyday lives are influenced by the foreign policies of the powerful West, multinational corporations, the need to move to find work, and by global media. These shifts and changes can remove some of the power and privileges that men have enjoyed in different regions and in slightly different ways. Peasant cultures, in which masculinity was based around owning land and controlling one's own work, have been all but obliterated by the spread of the all-powerful market. Unable to subsist in traditional ways many men have been forced to migrate to find work. As these globalization processes take hold, many men are likely to become increasingly aware of their subordinate status in relation to hegemonic masculinity. This can lead to men forcefully attempting to reassert their patriarchal privilege – at least in the domestic sphere. For example, some men in Iran and Afghanistan have tried to enforce strict controls over women. Others have turned to acts of terrorism to try to resist. Yet, also in the USA, some groups of largely white men are unhappy with social changes they see as bringing the loss of many privileges formerly enjoyed by men. They, too, turn to the domestic sphere to try to reassert privilege, forming movements such as the Promise Keepers, a Christian-based movement that supports very conservative views of men's proper role as breadwinner and family head, while women are enjoined to stay home and care for husband and children. These are attempts to reconfirm forms of masculinity that are marginalized in new ways within a new world order (Connell 2005; Kimmel 2005). But marginalization does not always produce reactionary retreats like those in these examples – it can potentially promote more positive resistance to gender norms.

Gayness can be seen as a resistance of hegemonic masculinity, especially given that dominant masculinity is based on homophobia, and being as far from feminine as possible (Connell 1995; Plummer 1999). Being camp does take on aspects of femininity, but more than that it has been seen as 'involving a positive aesthetic sensibility: a sense of beauty, and a sense of pain' (Segal 1990: 145). However, some gay men have also adopted macho identities, wearing lots of leather, building up their muscles, and so on (Segal 1990: 149–150). Gay men are not necessarily radically resisting traditional ways of doing gender and many can be very 'straight' in that respect (Connell 1995).

Men, whatever their sexuality, can and do change (Segal 1990) and some have been sympathetic to feminism. From the 1970s onwards, some men have tried to make changes and rethink their masculinity via men's groups, but as Segal (1990: 281) puts it, '[m]en in men's groups were quite often men in a muddle'. They were often guilty and not sure whether to support women or to transform or 'liberate' themselves by resisting traditional ways of being manly. Some were pro-feminist, but others were much less sympathetic towards women. Michael Messner (1997) sets out eight major forms of *organized* response by men to a perceived 'crisis' in the gender order. That 'crisis' consisted of social changes (including feminist movement) that have prompted men to examine masculinity as problematic rather than being able to take it for granted as something natural. I will not discuss all eight, but they are: men's liberation, men's rights, radical feminist men, socialist feminist men, men of colour, gay male liberationists, Promise Keepers, and the mythopoetic men's movement.

Messner (1997) has analysed these varieties of the 'politics of masculinities' in terms of their responses to the three major aspects of masculinities. First, he determines whether or not a particular group recognizes that men as a group enjoy 'institutionalized privileges' (for example, better jobs, higher social status) at the expense of women. The Promise Keepers, as mentioned above, are likely to defend the kind of privileges that men enjoy as 'right' and 'natural'. Radical feminist men, on the other hand, are highly critical of a system that allows men such privileges, and seek to change it. Second, Messner considers what kind of position the different groups take on 'the costs of masculinities'. Those costs are the negative effects that result from adhering to social expectations about masculinity. Messner argues that with privilege comes problems; because of expectations that they be 'in control' emotionally and physically, men's relationships and health suffer and they die younger. Groups like the mythopoetic movement focus on these costs. Their solution is to go off to beat drums in the forest and rediscover the 'real' man within (see Bly 1990). Those groups orientated to men's rights are also likely to emphasize these costs; recent fathers' rights groups protesting against custody being awarded to mothers are one example. Pro-feminists (radical and socialist feminist men) tend to deny the significance of costs of masculinity and focus on how women are usually disadvantaged and men usually privileged. Finally, Messner explores the importance to different groups of thinking about differences and/or inequalities among men. For gay male liberationists and men of colour these differences and inequalities are crucial. They do not share in the kinds of privileges available to straight and white men, and have not enjoyed the comfort of being able to take their masculinity for granted. Men's liberationists, in comparison, have tended to promote unity between men in striving to create an anti-sexist movement that would liberate men from the negative, woman-harming roles they had learned.

Often men's attempts to resist have failed to bring widespread change because, unlike most feminist activity, they have been personalized solutions to systemic problems. Much masculinity politics has focused on how men can change themselves in order to feel better. Pro-feminist (including radical feminist, socialist feminist) and anti-violence men's groups have been most likely to work towards the need for wider social change in order for gender inequalities to be addressed effectively (Connell 1995; Messner 1997).

CRITICALLY EVALUATING RESISTANCE

The effectiveness of the forms of gender politics discussed so far is difficult to measure, but can be critically discussed. I want to add to this a consideration of other forms of resistance not discussed, or only touched on. These forms of gendered resistance can include people changing their appearance and queer politics, by which people might find ways to 'undo' gender.

Measuring success

It is tempting to think either that feminism has achieved equality for women, or that it has largely been a failure, with most of the world's women still highly disadvantaged comparative to men. Similarly, the defence of hegemonic masculinity in the face of feminist challenges was thought to have taken on new strength during the late 1980s, with the emergence of a 'backlash' against many of the advances women had made (Faludi 1991).

Feminists were demanding better lives for women. They wanted women to have better education, better jobs with better pay, more control over whether or when to have children, and good childcare for those who wished to continue work while raising children. Certainly there have been many positive changes for women since Victorian times, and especially in the last half of the twentieth century. In the Western world girls are doing better at high school and over half of undergraduates at university are women. Equal pay legislation was passed in most wealthy nations in the 1970s and the gendered pay gap appears to be slowly but steadily closing. In some nations women's wages are close to 90 per cent of the average male wage (Holmes 2007b: 6–9). Women's reproductive choices are arguably greater, with most having better access to contraception and other forms of family planning than in the past (see Goldin and Katz 2002). Fertility technology such as in-vitro fertilization also allows women to conceive without a sexual partner, and can enable otherwise infertile couples to have children. Most mothers of dependent children are now in the workforce, although many work part-time (see, for example, Australian Bureau of Statistics 2007; Boushey 2007).

Many of these gains have not been widely enjoyed, or have slipped away. Globally female illiteracy is high and access to even basic education is often worse for girls than boys. Even in India, which provides more, and more equal, education than, say, most West and Central African nations, only 73 per cent of girls attend primary school compared to 80 per cent of boys (UNICEF 2006: 121). Worldwide, women are still earning only around 60 per cent of men's average wage (Connell 2002: 2; United Nations Statistics Division 2005). Abortion has also become more heavily restricted again in some nations – for example, the United States (Wind 2006). As mentioned above, access to decent paid or unpaid childcare remains limited in many affluent nations, especially with many grandmothers in the workforce (Crompton and Lyonette 2006; Kimmel 2006; Pocock 2006).

As I discussed in Chapter 3, Sylvia Walby (1997) suggests that, despite many changes for the better, women continue to be disadvantaged within what remains a male-dominated society. Although many women are less dependent on husbands and fathers, the public world of work and politics still has few women in positions of power. Patriarchy has not disappeared, but it has changed, and the kinds of problems faced by different groups of women and men have altered. The responses to those problems are also different, arguably focusing more on self-change than collective resistance.

Fashioning the self: individualization and resistance

Many of the current big names in sociology, such as Anthony Giddens, Zygmunt Bauman, and Ulrich Beck and Elisabeth Beck-Gernsheim, have been saying that we now live in a globalized world in which the traditional ways in which everyday social life was organized have broken down, or lost their power. Core forms of social support that people have formerly relied upon are not always available to them. People may live distantly from their extended family, grandparents may be too busy working to help care for grandchildren. The welfare state has been rolled back so benefits may be difficult to get. This means that people are forced to make their own decisions and choices. This 'institutionalized individualism' (Beck and Beck-Gernsheim 2002) has weakened the ties that formerly bound certain groups of people together and often served as the foundation for collective political resistance such as the class politics that produced unions and the politics of gender that fuelled feminism.

There are arguments that individualization has extended to women (Beck and Beck-Gernsheim 2002), but most women are still devoting large portions of their lives to caring for others. How they do this has been altered by shifts in the global economy. For example, in America it has become common for both partners to work, but men appear not to be doing much housework and only a little more childcare than they used to. Tired of combining paid work with a 'second shift' (Hochschild 1989) of housework, women who can afford it are hiring in domestic help. The women nannies and maids come to them from poorer countries and often leave their own children behind with female relatives in order to earn enough money overseas to save their family from poverty. This leaves a care gap and does not change the gendered division of labour; it just shifts the care work onto different groups of women (see Hochschild and Ehrenreich 2004). This clearly impacts on the everyday lives of people who become connected through these economies of care, as is explored in the recent film *Babel*. An American mother shot in Morocco can eventually be helicoptered to safety. The resources and power used to 'save' that one individual seem almost obscenely vast compared to the little available to the young Moroccan boy who shot her. And others pay a price, too, as revealed by the story of the Mexican nanny looking after the injured woman's American children. Her powerlessness becomes clear when she struggles to re-cross the American border after taking the children with her to Mexico so she can attend her own son's wedding. The vulnerability of individuals in the face of such global forces makes many turn to working on the self to try to gain some sense of control.

According to Charles Lemert and Anthony Elliott (2006), people's responses to individualism and globalization are necessarily focused on trying to make themselves the sort of individual thought to be desirable in their world. However, there is not simply one sort of desirable individual, but highly gendered ideas about how to look and act. For many women, ideals of a slim, pretty femininity are promoted through various social institutions they encounter in everyday life. As young girls, families and the school system give them messages about how to be. In the workplace subtle pressure or actual rules may be applied telling women how to dress and behave. And, in addition, the mass media daily present airbrushed and digitally altered images of impossibly thin and perfect women. As Susan Bordo (1989, 1993) suggests, this focus on being slender and white is what is presently thought 'normal' in the West. She therefore believes that it is possible to explain some of the new disorders afflicting primarily women as attempts to conform in an extreme fashion to these gender expectations, and yet also to resist them. Anorexia, for example, is an unconscious protest against gender expectations that discourage women from eating and make them feel ashamed of their appetites. It also carries to the extreme norms about femininity that exhort women to constantly work on their bodies to conform to ideals of feminine appearance. Anorexia shows how devotion to following those norms can be self-destructive, and therefore illustrates how unrealistic they are. Yet most anorexics will claim that they have no desire to look like the models in magazines. What they are doing can be read as a rejection of the way in which women's bodies are constantly sexualized and gazed upon. Anorexics are, one might say, literally trying to make their bodies go away. This may be a form of resistance, but tends to reinforce rather than challenge women's subjection to medical and media surveillance (Bordo 1989).

Nevertheless the centrality given to bodily appearance in judging women's worthiness and abilities leaves few choices but to turn to alteration of their bodies to try to give them a sense of greater control over their lives. The alterations extend from dieting to going to the gym to visiting beauty salons to undergoing cosmetic surgery (Davis 1995; Gimlin 2001; Black 2004). In slightly different ways these authors and others note that this 'body work' is a form of shopping, and like shopping the sense of anticipation accompanying buying something new is often followed by a vague feeling of disappointment. The new shirt/ nose/face cream has not made you into a different person, it has not solved your problems. Rather then give up on expecting consumption to fulfil their needs and desires, women try again: buy a different shirt or face cream; maybe the nose was not the problem, get the chin done. And it is not surprising that they do so, when to not play this body game leaves them open to harsh criticism, and to the likelihood of unemployment and social isolation. What women look like is taken to indicate the sort of person they are. If they fail to do sufficient work to attain the right look they are likely to be judged lazy, slovenly, promiscuous and just plain 'bad' (see Chapter 2).

Men are not free from these processes, as Susan Faludi (1999) has argued in her book *Stiffed: The Betrayal of the Modern Man*. She suggests that as socio-economic change has occurred in which Western nations have shifted from a manufacturing to a service base, men's traditional forms of employment have disappeared. Meanwhile women have been entering the workforce and, with the help of social changes fought for by feminists, have achieved greater independence. This has combined to leave men without their traditional role of breadwinner and without a clearly defined new role. Within a service-based economy and a consumer society the right kinds of bodies and 'personality' are crucial to success, as sociologists from C. Wright Mills (1956) to Mike Featherstone

(1991) have pointed out. Thus for many men the kinds of qualities that they expected to be valued for, such as rationality, reliability, emotional restraint and the ability to protect others, are no longer marketable. Instead they find themselves working on their 'six pack', starting a skincare regime, getting a back wax. Even, or especially, more privileged men may feel the need to turn to things such as cosmetic surgery to keep competitive within a labour market that no longer offers jobs for life (Lemert and Elliott 2006).

If a marketable look is essential within contemporary life, then it is not surprising that having the 'right' kind of clothes should be considered vital. In Chapter 2, I explained how having the 'right' kind of clothes is difficult for working-class women – and indeed men. Not just because of cost, but because the upper classes will move on to something new if 'the masses' adopt fashion items. Because of their wealth and power it is those upper classes whose ideas about what to wear dominate in 'good' jobs. It is hard for those not in the upper classes to know what the 'right' look is. Even if an individual manages to adopt a respectable look, they often feel that someone is bound to find them out (Skeggs 1997).

Meryl Storr (2002) discusses similar ideas about the importance of dress in how people make class distinctions, but her study of lingerie parties also gives a sense of the everyday small ways in which people resist class (and other) hierarchies. The lingerie parties have the same principles as Tupperware parties: a party organizer gets commission for gathering women and persuading them to buy underwear and sex toys from the Ann Summers range. Storr observed Ann Summers parties and interviewed party organizers. She argues that even though underwear is not usually on public display it can be used as a means of class distinction – especially 'lingerie'. The choices people make more often reinforce rather than upset class distinctions and related gender hierarchies. 'Lingerie' is aspired to by working- and lower-middle-class women as luxury. However, the kind of lingerie that Ann Summers sells tends to be frowned upon by the middle classes as 'tacky' and too overtly sexual. It is likely to imitate corsetry or bondage gear, have a good deal of lace, come in red, or involve leopardskin prints. Yet the working-class women who attend the lingerie parties see the underwear on offer as something 'special'. Sarah, a 31-year-old party organizer, says of her customers that 'they want to find, like a nice bit of quality lingerie, . . . rather than the usual cheap bits from down the road' (Storr 2002: 30). The women at the parties also distinguish themselves from 'snobbish', 'pretentious' and 'boring' wealthier women who, as organizers say, 'don't want people knowing that they've bought things from Ann Summers' and don't spend (Storr 2002: 32). Little did you think of the revolutionary potential of lacy knickers. But how revolutionary is this? The women may be resisting middle-class definitions of good taste with the more brothel-like styles of Ann Summers they see as sexy, fun and luxurious. However, their choice does not change the dominant system of values in which their taste is seen as bad. By displaying this taste through their clothing they are open to the judgements of others, and the powerful are likely to judge them as 'not the right kind of women' for important jobs or other social rewards.

As Joanne Finkelstein (1996) argues, what clothes say is open to interpretation, and they can often carry messages of both resistance and conformity. Women's fashion in many ways illustrates their social subordination, restraining them in tight-fitting clothing and uncomfortable shoes. Nevertheless it can be used by women to go against notions of passivity and express their individuality. In the late nineteenth and early twentieth century, Finkelstein notes, if women wore trousers it was seen as a highly rebellious act. In the late twentieth century, punk women's clothing, with ripped or fishnet stockings, tartan skirts and Doc Marten boots, is another example of a trend that rejected conventional feminine prettiness and was meant to signal a more aggressive style of feminine individuality. And women may also choose more conventional clothing to further their desires. Sometimes women may carefully exploit sexualized clothing to help them get what they want. It is also true that individuals can use fashion to 'get ahead' in the working world. If they can learn and adapt their clothing to emulate the styles of the powerful it may help them do well. However, there is the danger of getting it 'wrong', which may bring ridicule from those 'in the know'. And the powerful are still largely men. Putting on a suit does not automatically turn women into company directors and bring changes in gendered power relations, as various authors illustrate in a book called *Heading Nowhere in a Navy Blue Suit* (Kedgley and Varnham 1993). Neither is the gendered order overthrown by a man in a skirt.

Yet there is a general fashioning of the self (Finkelstein 1991) that goes with the increased importance put on appearances. Michel Foucault (e.g. 1980) has argued that with the development of modern forms of power it is no longer external force, but individual discipline that shapes people. People internalize social norms and try to discipline their bodies and selves accordingly. As well as diet and exercise they learn to like new styles of dress and furniture, and take on new ideas about the world. Although this can evoke a picture of docile bodies, Foucault says that the process always involves resistance. There is always a struggle involved in the making of social selves. However, some suggest that, for a woman, the process of fashioning a self involves thinking mostly about how other people see her, and in particular how men see her as a sex object (Mulvey 1975). This is not necessarily passive because there are contradictions in discourses of femininity. This can be seen in how those discourses are played out through the media, as Rabine notes in a study of women's magazines:

> On the one hand, women are given images of themselves as confident, free, and sexually powerful individuals who can display these qualities through their skilful use of clothing and cosmetics. On the other hand, during the last two decades, these same fashion magazines have published reports of women's submission and vulnerability, with articles on domestic violence, increasing rape rates, salary inequalities, sexual

harassment in the workplace, and other events and practices which illustrate that women are merely objects in a man's world.

(Rabine 1994, cited in Finkelstein 1996: 47–48)

If outer appearances have become increasingly seen as an expression of an inner self, women must therefore struggle to represent themselves as independent and serious individuals. In fact, Simmel argues that women adhere more to fashion because they receive social rewards from avoiding displays of individualism (cited in Finkelstein 1996: 42). Finkelstein (1996: 44) notes that this tends to ignore how '[i]deas about femininity and masculinity have changed as quickly as the garments'. Fashion changes are driven partly by the economic viability of new ideas and partly by shifts in perception assisted, but not driven by, advertising as it stirs up desire. The self-fashioning only ever approximates to the ideal and thus its pleasures are limited, says Finkelstein. Although women may actively self-fashion, it is argued that they do so to satisfy the male gaze and that this reinforces their lack of power. However, some feminists have proposed that women can resist a passive femininity by reading images and texts 'against the grain' (Betterton 1987) and that there is a 'female gaze' (see Gamman and Marshment 1988) through which women can see themselves and men.

I have already argued that men have become recognized more as a group who are subject to the 'sex sells' mantra. Men's self-fashioning has historically shifted from an emphasis on exhibiting his own wealth via his person, to using his wife and children to display success. This has slowly altered as more women enter the world of work and express themselves (Finkelstein 1996: 48–50). Sexualized images of men are now more common. I mentioned the Diet Coke advertisement above; writing this during a short stay in New Zealand, another striking example is provided by the huge billboards featuring All Blacks rugby player, Dan Carter, looking splendid in the Jockey underpants he models, with his highly toned abdominal muscles on display. Another example is the latest homage to actress Ursula Andress in a James Bond film. In the first Bond film, in the 1960s, a shot of Andress emerging from the sea in the newly invented bikini was highly sexual for the time. Halle Berry repeated a version of it in a Bond movie earlier this century, reinforcing the woman-as-sex-object theme. However, in the most recent Bond film, starring Daniel Craig, it is Bond himself who is filmed coming out of the sea dripping wet, in his tight swimming trunks. Of course, these images may appeal to some men as well as to women, but they do seem to indicate a small shift that recognizes women's desires in a more active way.

Although women have achieved greater independence, it is often argued (e.g. Wolf 1990; and see Finkelstein 1996) that fashion distracts women from more serious pursuits and undermines their capacity to resist oppression, perhaps because gender hierarchies continue to be reinforced. It is argued that, despite constant changes in feminine and masculine dress, gender differences continue to be reinforced; the cut of men's versus women's trousers and shirts differs, for example. Femininity and masculinity remain thought of and usually 'done' as though they were opposite and mutually exclusive ways of being.

Queer theory tries to break down the dichotomy between masculine and feminine. Foremost in this was a highly influential book by Judith Butler, published in 1990 (see Chapter 2). In it Butler argues against the idea that femininity and masculinity are 'natural' and opposing categories. We need to cause 'gender trouble' (as the book is called) by breaking down the boundaries between genders. She gives the example of how drag does this because it 'plays upon the distinction between the anatomy of the performer and the gender that is being performed' (Butler 1990: 137). A male drag queen is imitating femininity or a woman cross-dresser is mimicking masculinity, and by doing so they show that sex and gender are distinct. You do not have to have female biology to act in feminine ways. Butler is following Foucault, extending his ideas to show that power produces us as the kind of *gendered* individuals that we are. Ways of thinking about gender as mapping onto 'natural' sex categories (female = feminine, male = masculine) are internalized by individuals and make them into girls and boys who become women and men. As soon as a doctor/midwife says 'it's a girl' the gender system of power is brought into action to start creating that baby as a girl. The point for Butler is that there is no in-between option; no neutral form of human being. If we do not know someone's gender we do not know how to treat them. The problem with the feminine/masculine dichotomy for Butler and other queer theorists is that it restricts more fluid expressions of desire. The girl/boy dichotomy is heterosexist, it assumes that girls will grow up and love boys and have more little girls and boys. Homosexual or more bisexual or shifting sexual pleasures are hence seen as 'unnatural'.

According to queer theory, gender can be resisted by queering, or messing up, gender boundaries. From this a more fluid flow of desire and of identities becomes possible, a diversity that will resist heteronormativity (the idea that heterosexuality is natural and normal). This can be seen in TV shows like *Will and Grace* where gay/straight identities are not always clear, but does gender get reinforced (they become mums and dads in the end)? If the categories 'feminine' and 'masculine' can be played with, this questions their supposed naturalness. Thinking about gender identities as fluid instead of fixed opens up new possibilities for whom and how we love. Doing gender in ways that draw on aspects of both femininity and masculinity might be possible, but it is not certain that it really helps break down gender binaries. And some of the ways in which homosexual identities are performed can reinforce gender differences. I will talk more about the possibilities of a queer future in the next chapter, but discussing it here recognizes how it can challenge and change the sex/gender system. It is a radical form of resistance, which considers how to fundamentally alter the way in which gender is socially organized. I want to finish by summarizing forms of resistance in terms of those that propose individual change, those that encourage reforms to the present system and those that envisage a different gender order.

SUMMARY

Individualized forms of politics focusing on altering aspects of one's self can bring changes for the person involved but do not typically alter the patterns of gender domination that exist. One example touched on in this chapter is that of a man who is drawn by the mythopoetic movement and joins a group that helps him explore the 'warrior within'. This is an urban modern male fantasy of a 'primitive' society in which men (and women) were closer to nature and supposedly certain of their place in the world. It is an invented version of a way of life that may never have actually existed as it is imagined, but it is presented as the 'real' form of masculinity rather than as one way to be masculine that, if it ever existed, was based on specific historical and cultural conditions. In some sense those conditions made people be 'closer to nature', given that the kinds of life imagined are of subsistence cultures where human communities had to understand and carefully use their environment in order to survive. The notion that men's brute strength was key to that survival, whether as hunters or warriors, is debateable. If it is hunter-gatherer societies that are being imagined then it is women's gathering, which was hard physical work, that provided most of the food in such societies (Slocum 1975). Men banging drums in the forest in imitation of some made-up vision of the wild man within is not something that addresses the realities of gendered divisions of labour past or present. Harking back to notions of a 'natural' masculinity tends to be a way in which men can avoid change. 'This is just how I am,' they say, 'I have to be true to myself.' And nothing changes.

Reformist politics, including various versions of the liberal feminist politics set out first by Mary Wollstonecraft, suggest that the social system needs reforming. They resist women's oppression by insisting that given the same opportunities as men women can gain social equality. However, it tends to be more elite women who have benefited from these reforms. Education and work opportunities have not advanced as much for most ordinary women. And these types of resistance assume that masculine models of success are adequate, rather than rethinking what is valued.

Radical resistance is often judged to be highly threatening to the social order and is punished accordingly. It is threatening because, by definition, what is radical questions the basic principles around which society is organized. Radical resistance to gender therefore does imagine a completely different kind of society in which differences between women and men would be less significant, or perhaps not significant at all. These are imaginings of possible futures of gender, which I explore more fully in the next chapter.

5

THE FUTURE OF GENDER

INTRODUCTION

Shiny metallic surfaces and clean, cold, pill-eating androgynous beings were images from one version of the future popular in the twentieth century. Imagining the future has been an important aspect of social life in all cultures as peoples try to make sense of the meaning of their life and think about the world in which their children and grandchildren will live. By looking at history sociologists have found compelling illustrations of the way in which that world changes. Older people in many societies find themselves often living in a world almost unimaginably different from the one they inhabited in their early years. One of the most disorientating changes appears to be in what it means to be feminine or masculine and in how women and men act. Watching men's hair get longer and women's shorter, seeing women working in a range of jobs previously reserved for men – these and many other small details and large alterations accumulate and combine to make gender a different set of everyday practices than it was for the generation before. For most grandmothers of today's young women it was unthinkable to go to town without gloves and a hat.

Those currently grandfathers were not expected to be present at the birth of their children, in fact often they were shooed away. Today fathers change nappies and push prams. Young women dress rather less formally. Presently, boundaries between genders are changing and arguably becoming increasingly blurred. One of the latest instances is the rise of the metrosexual. This is a type of man who differs from more macho versions of masculinity. He is more likely to be thin than muscly; more concerned with face cream than footy. However, much imagining of the future assumes that women and men will not become more alike, but continue to differ. This is also true of many past imaginings of what lies ahead.

It is possible to talk of a history of the future because there have been a variety of previous visions of what the future holds. These tell us a great deal about the social world from which they have emerged, as well as about what is to come. Beginning with a history of futures this chapter touches on early sociological thoughts about where the world was headed, limited though they were in relation to gender. More possibilities were portrayed by science fiction writers, especially those with some interest in social and political analysis, especially in women's emancipation. These represent some of the best efforts to envision alternatives to our present ways of doing and thinking about gender. I look at some examples from New Zealand politician Julius Vogel in the nine-teenth century, and from feminist sci-fi writers connected to the second wave. In some regards, science fiction has become part of our present lives as we live in a weird world where technology can reshape our bodies in hitherto unimagined ways. The implications of the rise of the cyborg for sex/gender categories and boundaries are considered. Two contrasting propositions are then presented, which provide both comparison and a critical angle on gendered futures. One set of debates imagines a future in which gender boundaries are blurred, messed up, or queered. Another view sees tradition as not having entirely lost its force, and notes that there are areas in which gender boundaries are being reinforced in restrictive ways. Finally, this chapter considers the currently pervasive concern about the future in which climate change may bring major changes to everyday life and ways of doing gender.

A HISTORY OF FUTURES

Sociological imaginings

The man who coined the word 'sociology', nineteenth-century French philosopher Auguste Comte, was specifically interested not just in understanding everyday social life in the present, but in using that understanding to create a better future. For him, sociology was the ultimate science, one that would provide an accurate understanding of humanity that could bring about a more moral and ordered society (Comte 1974/1853). This was a conservative vision of the future in which hierarchies were seen as crucial to maintaining order. Comte's views on women varied during his life, but he basically thought women and men different by nature, and imagined a future in which women would be 'freed' from having to struggle to meet their material needs and able to focus on their 'proper' role of caring for others. He wished to see them without responsibilities in the public sphere of work and political decision making. However, his contemporary, the English sociologist Harriet Martineau, had different views (Hoecker-Drysdale 2003).

Martineau was a remarkable woman and her translation of Comte, along with her other copious publications, was crucial in helping bring sociology to Britain and the rest of the English-speaking world. However, she differed from him substantially in how she saw differences between the sexes. Comte believed men within social elites should rule in the social order of the future. Martineau wanted women to have the opportunity to fully participate in society. Her views on women are recognizably sociological in that she saw social constraints such as lack of education, lack of financial independence and lack of political power as what made women's lives different from men's. For instance, in her detailed study of the newly formed democracy of America, she was highly critical of women's lack of political status and hoped they would soon have a vote (Martineau 1837). Social constraints were things that could be changed and she did agree with Comte in believing that social scientific methods could and should be used to gain knowledge that would be the basis of constructing a better society (Hoecker-Drysdale 2003).

The key founding fathers of sociology, Karl Marx, Max Weber and Emile Durkheim, also envisioned a better future but had little to say about how gender relations might change. They were men of their age in seeing progress as central to modernity. They were rather less convinced than others that progress was inevitably positive. Durkheim was perhaps most sanguine in this respect. All tended to characterize relations between women and men as natural, not constructed. Indeed, as Sydie (1987) has argued, these early sociologists generally accepted the thinking of the time in which women's lower social position was explained as resulting from their closer association to nature. Women's reproductive capacities supposedly rendered them unable to engage in the rational thought and action deemed necessary for active participation in the public sphere. Therefore they had to be dependent on men, and men's control over them was typically thought justified. This assumes that the public world of paid work and political decision making is what constitutes culture. As feminists (see Chapters 3 and 4) have long suggested, this devalues the importance of women's unpaid caring work within the family and its contribution to the stability and continuance of the social world. Marx, Weber and Durkheim (and Comte) did at least think a little about women's place in the home and its social importance.

Marx's focus was on capitalism, and in imagining the future he believed that women would gain a measure of equality as they increasingly entered the paid workforce (Sydie 1987: 90). This was based on a thorough examination of women's subordinate social position as firmly tied to the way the privatized family emerged within a capitalist society. Marx himself made notes on this, but it was his friend and co-writer Engels (1985/1884) who put together the final analysis of *The Origin of the Family, Private Property and the State*. The argument is that the form of family life in which women are dependent on men has come about as a consequence of capitalism. Put simply, as society has become more settled, initially around agriculture, surplus wealth has emerged. Within capitalism, that wealth has become concentrated in the hands of individual men (capitalists who own the new factories and businesses). Those men have become concerned about handing on their wealth to their children. In order to be sure that it is their children to whom they are leaving their inheritance, men begin to more strictly control women, especially by keeping them dependent within the family. Based on this logic, it is clear why Marx and Engels would suggest that women would require the economic independence attained by paid work to gain equality. Although Marx believed that women's equality was crucial to socialism, it was thought to be something that was of secondary importance to class struggle. Come the revolution, women would be equal.

Weber's overall vision of a social future is decidedly less revolutionary; he fails to imagine gender inequalities as social constructions, and therefore he assumes that they will continue. He saw men as 'naturally' the physical and intellectual superiors of women (Sydie 1987: 59). However, his analysis of patriarchal power is important in making sense of women's social status. Weber clearly sets out the operation of patriarchy as a traditional form of power in which elder males within families exercise control over younger males and over women (Sydie 1987). His characterization of that form of power sees it as fundamentally working within households, whereas outside the household an individual patriarch's power is limited by having to negotiate with other men. This does not contribute to really understanding the power relations between men and women (Sydie 1987: 84–85). Feminists have developed the notion of patriarchy to refer not to the rule of older males, but to a society in which men have the power to dominate women (see Walby 1990). Other ideas of Weber's can perhaps give some insight into how women have managed to gain some power, although it is uncertain whether this will progress in the future. Weber (1968/1921, 1981/1927) is famous for his arguments that society has been subject to a process of rationalization that has seen calculation and rules dominate social organization. The world becomes 'disenchanted' as modern ideas emphasize the importance of using science and reason to understand it, instead of superstition and religion. We can take from this that it becomes more difficult to justify men's power over women in traditional terms or in terms of it being God's will. However, not only ideas but the way society is organized would need to change in order to ease or erase gender inequalities.

Durkheim (1933/1893), in his work on *The Division of Labour in Society*, argues that as society became more specialized and the division of labour more complex, the 'natural' differences between women and men would increase. He did not view this as negative, but as something that would contribute to the smooth functioning of society. As a functionalist Durkheim saw the various parts of social life as each having a function or purpose in maintaining the social order. Women, he noted, had increasingly retired to the private world of family life to specialize as carers, and this he thought a proper and sensible reflection of their 'natural' abilities. If women did become more active within society, he thought they would take on different roles to men, ones to which they were supposedly fitted by nature (Sydie 1987: 32). With a slight variation, this view was taken up and expanded by other functionalists such as Parsons (Parsons and Bales 1956), who argued that complex modern society required people to specialize in either the 'expressive' skills required to socialize children or the 'instrumental' (goal orientated) skills required in the competitive public world of work. Parsons thought that it was socialization rather than 'nature' that fitted women for the expressive and men for the instrumental roles (Connell 2002: 123), but he did not imagine the possibility that men could be socialized to be more expressive and women to be instrumental. In this, like Durkheim, he affirmed gender inequalities instead of critically challenging them. More radical alternative visions of how women and men might be in the future were better found elsewhere.

Science fiction futures of gender

At the turn of the nineteenth into the twentieth century, sociology was still a small speck in the intellectual landscape, but visions of the future of gender were found in fictional writings. These imaginings are of necessity very much located in their own time and driven by the issues and concerns of the days in which they were written. Yet for this very reason they are extremely revealing insights into how gender differences both persist and change.

One example is a novel written in 1889 that imagines our present as a time in which women hold high political office and virtually all forms of gender discrimination have been removed. *Anno Domini 2000, or Woman's Destiny* was written by former New Zealand Prime Minister Julius Vogel, after his retirement to England. Vogel was highly progressive in his political ideals, which included support for women's rights and for some form of what we now call a welfare state. Nevertheless he is very Victorian in explaining why women are so prominent in government in his fictional version of the year 2000:

> . . . woman has become the guiding, man the executive, force of the world. Progress has necessarily become greater because it is found that women bring to the aid of more subtle intellectual capabilities faculties of imagination that are the necessary adjuncts of improvement. The arts and caprices which in the old days were called feminine proved to be the silken chains fastened by men on women to lull them into inaction. Without abating any of their charms, women have long ceased to submit to be the playthings of men. They lead men, as of yore, but not so much through the fancy or the senses as through the legitimate

consciousness of the man that in following woman's guidance he is
tending to higher purposes.

(Vogel 2000/1889: 36)

In other words, men should recognize that women are morally
superior, and thus more fit to run the world. This is based on
nineteenth-century arguments, which some feminists also put
forward, that women should be given the vote and other political
power because they were naturally fitted as nurturers to be moral
guardians (see Rendall 1985). Although this argument was very
helpful in convincing people at the time that women should have
a more active role within society, it had limitations. In particular it
based women's rights to power on a view of them as pure, asexual
and mothering. This had quite strong class connotations, so that
only 'respectable' (that is, middle class) women were really seen
as fit to be citizens and to exercise power. These kind of views
continue to echo in ways that make it difficult for all women in
politics to express their sexuality while maintaining political cred-
ibility (Holmes 2000a). Vogel does try to appreciate the possibility
of women being passionate sexually as well as politically capable,
and creates women characters who fall in love, marry and still
become Prime Minister. However, these characters are all from an
elite class and have, or attain, considerable wealth. And they
remain very recognizably women.

Many visions of the future of gender still assume there to be
some kind of fundamental differences between women and men.
Julius Vogel (2000/1889) imagines a politically important
Emperor who reigns over a United British Empire that is a feder-
ated collection of self-governing states. A crisis emerges over controversy about whether or not to remove the last remaining legal
discrimination against women: the preferential succession of male
heirs to the crown. The young male Emperor objects, not because
he doubts women's abilities to rule, but because he believes that
the Emperor must be capable of leading the army. In the Epilogue,
Vogel as author shows that this argument is not sufficient:

What annoyed [the Emperor] most was the fallacy of his own arguments long ago. It will be remembered that he had laid chief stress on the probability that the female succession would reduce the chance of the armies being led by the Emperor in person in case of war. But it was certain that if his son succeeded, he would not head the army in battle. . . . he had no taste for military knowledge . . . and it was certain he never would become a great general.

(Vogel 2000/1889: 174)

The more capable older sister is, to everyone's relief, finally able to succeed, but there is no mention of her being a general. This is the point at which Vogel fails to imagine an extension or change to how gender is done. While men are not inevitably suited to be soldiers he fails to imagine that women might take on martial duties. Yet we cannot blame him for this in 1889, when in the twenty-first century debates continue over women's role in the military and especially over whether or not they should be on the front line (e.g. Wilgoren 2003). There are some assumptions being made about women as essentially non-violent.

Other fictional futures also assume that there will continue to be differences between women and men in terms of their supposedly 'natural' tendency to and aptitude for violence. Some second-wave feminist science fiction makes this central to its vision of the future. For example, in *The Wanderground* (Gearhart 1985) Mother Earth herself has revolted against the violence of men. 'Male' technology no longer operates outside the city and large numbers of women have left there to establish women-loving communities in the wilderness. There they develop their connections to each other and to the natural world. They are telepathic, and this includes 'talking' to animals. Some can also fly. They see their task as '*[t]o work as if the earth, the mother, can be saved*' (Gearhart 1985: 211, original emphasis). But this is more Utopian, along with Vogel. Others are more dystopian, and imagine men using force to gain firm control over women. In *The Handmaid's Tale*, Margaret Atwood (1986) creates a bleak future in which women have become entirely subservient to men. A passive femininity is debased by a misogynist macho masculinity, the emphasis on difference is seen as leading to a severe hierarchy in which women have no freedom. Atwood's vision is of these differences as not real, but as socially enforced by power and the use of violence.

The view that men are 'naturally' violent and women 'naturally' nurturing is one that sociologists dispute because they see those differences as socially created. As our social world changes, it is not just a matter of women and men adapting to that. What it means to be a woman or a man also changes. Even at present not all cultures have the same ideas about what is masculine or feminine, and these ideas change. Masculinity may become less associated with violence in the same way that Western understandings of feminine sexuality have completely altered. In the medieval period women were thought 'naturally' sexually insatiable, but later the Victorians portrayed them as 'naturally' sexually passive. How gender is understood alters and this means different differences between women and men may be emphasized in the future.

The polarization of sex/gender differences is not the only possibility for the future, and some have imagined worlds in which those differences do not exist, or disappear. These are perhaps the most radical, because they cause us to think about the artificiality of current gender categorizations. There are other ways it might be. One example is Ursula Le Guin's (1969) novel, *The Left Hand of Darkness*. In this world everyone is androgynous. No distinctions are made on the grounds of gender, and sex becomes evident only when a couple begin to copulate during a certain period of the hormonal cycle that all these people share. When they come together for coitus, each partner will take on a sexual form that complements the other's, but this emerges in their sexual interaction and is in no way predetermined by their anatomy. This may seem far-fetched, but already technological advancements are challenging sex/gender boundaries and indeed the very boundary of the human.

COMPARING FUTURES CRITICALLY: A CYBERING, QUEERING OR RETRADITIONALIZING OF GENDER?

Technology and gendered cyborgs

It is possible that technology and the impacts of human industry on the natural world may make sex, and potentially gender differences, disappear. In December 1996 the magazine *Science* published a story about hermaphrodite fish in a polluted river near London. The male fish had testes but were making eggs. This was found to be due to the large amounts of an oestrogen-like protein in the water. It is thought that such pollution could cause other species to become intersex, including humans (Kaiser 1996). But there are other ways in which technology and its social impacts may shape the future of gender.

Donna Haraway is a biologist turned philosopher of science who in the 1990s envisioned a future in which technology becomes ever more a part of human being. This future has already begun and Haraway (1985, 1997) claims that most human beings are already cyborgs. A cyborg is part machine, part human. Our everyday lives are lived as cyborgs because technology is constantly incorporated into and by our bodies. For example, people who have pacemakers inside them to regulate their hearts are part machine. Indeed, so are those with silicon breast implants. This second example gives some indication of how technology affects sex/gender.

Haraway (1985, 1997) is talking not just about surgical implants, but about all kinds of ways in which technology makes us gendered cyborgs. She mentions running shoes as a form of technology that shapes our bodies, but a more clearly gendered example might be bra technology. A highly artificial shaping of breasts is expected in the West. Even those women who do not have breast implants are still cyborgs because they employ considerable effort to make their breasts take the shape currently fashionable. In the 1950s, cone-shaped bras were popular, now a more spherical shape seems to be preferred, breasts are lifted high, made rounder and pushed together by a variety of 'push-up', padded, 'balcony' and 'wonder' bras.

It is not that technology is 'bad', but Haraway is trying to recognize and consider the implications for our identity of these joinings of human and machine. Potentially the way that technology makes bodies malleable can question the naturalness of distinctions between female and male and their relationships to feminine and masculine. Take bras again. There are special websites for transvestites and transsexuals, so that those who are shifting sex/gender categories can look the part. Here bras may come with false breasts included, underpants can be purchased that have hip padding to give male to female cross-dressers a more 'feminine' body shape. However, these are still examples of people trying to fit into one category or another. As noted above, it is also possible that technology may have intended and unintended consequences that blur gender. Anne Balsamo (2003) has suggested that gender is not simply blurred but dislocated by technology, and particularly by the way in which technology is used to monitor as well as shape bodies:

> Medical authorities encourage us to monitor consumption of sugar, caffeine, salt, fat, cholesterol, nicotine, alcohol, steroids, sunlight, narcotics, through the use of such devices as electronic scales, home pregnancy kits, diabetes tests, blood pressure machines and fat calipers.
>
> (Balsamo 2003: 54)

These ways of visualizing the body fragment it into parts and processes, so that gender identity is difficult to locate. Is womanliness in hips, lips, breasts or womb? If femininity comes naturally, why all the monitoring, all the effort? Gender becomes a shifting boundary marking a contested connection between the natural body and the way in which the body is made sense of culturally.

Haraway's (1997) vision of the future is one in which we can shift away from obsessions with blood and genes as the supposed basis of fixed categories like sex and its related label: gender. What she hopes for is a social order where categories are based on affinity, on who/what we feel we are like and who we like. Technoscience can cross the usual boundaries between categories and create new forms of life. If it operates with a sense of justice in mind then that future could be one in which there are no separate sexes, or there are several. However, technoscience presently tends to operate for profit. New life forms, like the genetically engineered mice known as Oncomouse, are created and then patented by science corporations. In terms of gender, though, it is FemaleMan that is of most interest.

FemaleMan is the author figure Haraway adopts because she is a disruption of gendered stories in which men dominate. She borrows this figure from Joanna Russ's feminist science fiction novel *The Female Man*, which charts the story of four genetically identical women from alternative realities. Their names all begin with J and together they symbolize the difficulties for women to be the heroes of a story. Haraway (1997: 75) says her FemaleMan is:

> a tool for provoking a little technical and political intercourse, or criminal conversation, or reproductive commerce, about what counts as nature, for whom, at what cost? This is the kind of conversation that prepares one for life in the narrative webs of the New World Order Inc., biopower, the Second Millenium, and the Net.

Tempting though the allure of an androgynous or gender-flexible cyborg is, there are those who caution against it. Braidotti (2001), for example, argues that the cyborg is still gendered, and recognizing this will help to avoid nostalgia for the pre-techno without falling for technological utopias. For Braidotti it is important to consider how technology can enhance the embodied subject. Yet she also argues that this enhancement should uphold the importance of the material body as flesh and not deny pain or mortality. Hurt and death are crucial to maintaining a sense of connection to others. If we are moving into 'post-humanity' where there is a sexual openness, care will be required so that 'the feminine' does not disappear. She is concerned that if sex/gender boundaries do blur they will do so by women becoming more 'male'. This raises questions about the deliberate shaping of sex/gender.

Sex can be made surgically, it is no longer simply determined by nature. This is one instance of how the boundary between what is natural and what is humanly created is broken down. Sex-change surgery has become fairly regular since the 1970s, although the first sex-change operation (male to female) was performed in Berlin in the 1930s (Meyerowitz 2002: 15). Technical limits are still important and the difficulties of constructing a penis make female to male sex change more problematic in many respects. Nevertheless, the possibility of sex change alters our notions of how much influence our bodies have over our gender identity. Some who are born male feel strongly that they are a woman trapped in a man's body. Throughout history there have been examples of biological women who have lived as men and biological men who have lived as women. However, only fairly recently has the technology existed to allow them to change their bodies to fit with their identity. The interesting question is why they feel that they need to make those changes. Why does a biological woman not feel she can express a masculine identity and desires with the body she has? Some women perhaps do and one option may be to take on a lesbian identity. However, there is a common-sense notion that a person's gender (feminine or masculine) should match their sex (female or male) and that it is opposites that attract. This has been challenged by queer theory.

Queer futures

One future imagined by the likes of Judith Butler (1990, 1993, 2004) and other queer theorists is the breaking down of the idea that masculine and feminine are stable and opposing identities. They want to blur the boundary between feminine and masculine. Queer theory is critical of **heteronormativity**, which is the dominance of social norms that suggest heterosexuality is the 'normal' and 'natural' form of sexuality. Sexual preferences are not seen as fixed and desires are not static. Identities are not understood in terms of being heterosexual versus homosexual, but are seen as much more multiple, fragmented and constantly shifting. Queer theory celebrates a radical diversity that encourages a free flow of desire without concerns about what sex/gender the object of desire is. Indeed the idea is that people can shift across sex/gender categories.

Heterosexuality and heteronormativity are questioned. To 'queer' things means to mess them up, to pull apart the straightness of the social world and encourage more playful and diverse ways of living pleasurable lives. There is some indication that heterosexual relations are becoming less central to social life as people adopt a range of ways of living (see Chapter 3; Roseneil 2000, 2005). Presently, however, heterosexuality is the foundation of sex/gender categories. Ideas about what it means to be a woman or a man are based on the assumption that opposites attract. We assume that girls will grow into feminine women who will love masculine men. It is presumed that they will consummate their love and reproduce little girls and boys, and the process will continue (Butler 1993, 2004). However, meanings can change, and so can gender identities. How we relate to whom has changed considerably since our grandparents' day and is likely to continue to change. Already non-heterosexual ways of life have become more socially acceptable and it may be that in future love will be expected to flow more freely without regard to the sex/gender of the beloved.

Queer theory has been criticized for being over-optimistic in predicting that sex/gender identities will become more fluid. This is thought to ignore the inequalities associated with marginalized identities such as being a woman or non-heterosexual. Deconstructing identities is thought to have limits and, in this view, reclaiming gay and lesbian identities is still seen as necessary. These identities are understood as flexible and diverse, but as restricted by the changing social context. Meanings attached to homosexuality are socio-historical products that usually constrain non-heterosexuals (Weeks 1985, 2000). It can also be argued that queer theory focuses too much on non-heterosexuals and that this does not really undermine sex/gender identities. It may be politically important to stress queer identities as legitimate alternatives to being straight, but heterosexuality done differently logically must have the potential to be part of more subversive ways of doing gender identity (Beasley 2005: 157, 170). And of course gays and lesbians are not inevitably going against mainstream ideas about sex and gender (Connell 1995) – for example, many lesbians gender each other as either butch (aligned with fairly stereotypical notions of macho) or femme (akin to stereotypes about femininity). Sometimes supposedly transgressive ways of doing sex/gender actually reinforce mainstream notions – for example, drag queens tend to do femininity in very stereotypical ways, overemphasizing stereotypes of femininity based on glamour, girlishness and frivolity (Jeffreys 1996). Both the cyborg and the queer future suggest a withering away of binary gender categories and the freeing of gender from tradition, but not all agree.

The detraditionalization or the retraditionalization of gender?

People no longer simply do what their parents did. Some key current debates within sociology focus on how tradition has declined and individuals have to create their own ways to live, including decisions about gender roles (e.g. Giddens 1990; Beck and Beck-Gernsheim 2002). These practices of constantly reshaping one's life based on the knowledge available are known as **reflexivity** and are part of processes of individualization that force people to take responsibility for their own lives. People may have more choices as old ways of doing things lose their hold, but individualization does not necessarily involve detraditionalization. John Thompson (1995), for instance, argues that traditional ways of doing things are no longer widely seen as guiding norms, nor does doing things traditionally automatically legitimate actions. The normative and legitimating aspects of tradition have been lost. However, he says that people still use tradition to make sense of the world and in forming identity. Lisa Adkins (2000) argues that tradition still constrains women. She thinks that, in some areas, gender is becoming retraditionalized. One of these areas is the workplace, where a new emphasis on family has emerged that restricts women. Adkins argues that economic changes have largely excluded women from new types of workplaces in which workers have more control over their work. Domestic and welfare changes also often push women back into traditional gender roles, as they take most of the responsibility for caring for children. Theorists have proposed that reflexivity and agency have increased within the realm of family and relationships (e.g. Giddens 1992; Beck and Beck-Gernsheim 1995) but research in this area continues to reveal the persistence of tradition in how women and men organize the emotional and household work within their intimate lives (see Chapter 3). However, there remain possibilities for women to do things differently.

The gendered nature of self and social construction can be challenged. According to Giddens, reflexivity extends to all areas of social life and is 'deeply unsettling' (1990: 30) because knowledge is constantly being revised and there is no certitude on which to base actions. It is this impossibility of relying on reason that produces an 'emotionalization of reflexivity' (Holmes 2007a). Under such conditions people take account of information, but their decisions and relations to others are heavily based on emotional reactions. Individuals will decide to 'go with a gut feeling', or their assessment of how reliable certain information is will be based on how much they trust the person who produced or delivered it. These emotional reactions are not necessarily irrational and are open to interpretation. The importance of interpreting emotions has been recognized in some realms such as in some social movements where emotional reflexivity is taught as a practice that is key to developing an active subject who can bring about social change (King 2006). Even within the supposedly highly rationalized realm of business, there has been attention to people's skills at interpreting others' emotions (King 2007). For instance, there was a fad at the turn of the twenty-first century for encouraging managers to learn 'emotional intelligence' to help them understand the needs of their staff and manage in a more caring fashion (e.g. Ryback 1997). Yet the technological world in which we live is liable to impact on how we experience and express emotions (Williams 1998), and indeed the consequences of technology may bring not only emotional disconnection or new ways of connecting, but new traumas, conflicts and disasters.

Globalization, climate change and the nature of gender

As we entered the new millennium there was considerable reflection on what might lie ahead, much of it concerned with processes of globalization. Various visions, popular and socio-logical, have emerged of a global society in which nation states cease to have significance, and populations are 'multi-ethnic, hybrid and culturally diverse' (Westwood 2000: 191). Utopian imaginings see the exciting possibilities, but some sociologists (e.g. Bauman 1998; Sassen 1998) are concerned with the destructive potential of already apparent trends towards increased ethnic con-flict, ecological disaster and the resulting mass displacement of persons. Such consequences are given fictional form in a book by P.D. James, made into the recent film *Children of Men*. In this near future the human race has become infertile and refugees battle for survival within a climate of repression, violence and despair. It is hinted in the film that a key element in bringing about such a future is environmental degradation.

As I write, current visions of the future are heavily focused on the likely outcomes of climate change. Social scientists have only recently joined the debates to consider how global warming might impact on society (e.g. Urry 2007; Lever-Tracy 2008). If climate change is as serious as some predictions foretell, then the whole way in which society is organized and the ways in which we live will be fundamentally changed (Lever-Tracy 2008). Urry (2007) suggests that two scenarios are likely. The first is one in which tribalism replaces complex societies as fires, desertification, flooding and other disasters related to climate change force mass migration and disorder. This regional warlordism will see a return to the local and a collapse of standards of living.

Although not explicitly stated, the tribal warlordism scenario conjures up a *Mad Max* vision of the future in which past patterns of gender return. These are patterns emphasizing masculinity as expressed through strength and the use of physical force to protect their own. It is not quite clear what might become of women in this world. Of course, this is not just science fiction. For reasons other than climate change this is similar to what happened in Afghanistan in the late twentieth century. The Taliban certainly conform to a model of tribal warlords instituting heavy restrictions on women over whom they gained authority. It is not Islamic beliefs that impose those restrictions (Afshar 1997) – note that the neighbouring, predominantly Muslim, Pakistan has had women such as Benazhir Bhutto prominent in political power struggles. Restrictions on women do appear to emerge within social conditions in which tradition is threatened *and* resources scarce. Pessimists might suggest that this presages a spread of new but historically recognizable forms of patriarchy in which fear and physical force are used to constrain women. Climate change has the potential to reduce advanced societies to the level of precarious survival, which the destabilization and poverty of a lengthy war with Soviet Russia brought to Afghanistan. Yet it is not clear that these conditions necessarily produce regimes oppressive to women. Rwanda had a similar history of recent tribal warfare but, as noted earlier, has emerged to have currently the world's best representation of women in its parliament, where near to 50 per cent of seats are occupied by women (Inter-parliamentary Union 2007) – some indication of more egalitarian gender relations emerging from a violent and impoverished past. Thus, a regional warlordism that oppresses women is by no means the inevitable outcome of global warming.

The other scenario climate change could bring about is one in which the planet is saved from self-destruction, but only by imposing strict controls upon the self and especially by digitizing the self – possibly in gendered ways. Already we microchip pets, and this may extend to people so that their carbon emissions can be tightly controlled. The movement of individuals would be digitally traced within a green panopticon. Strictly imposed carbon allowances would then function as a measure of worth and status (Urry 2007). No doubt there would be gendered aspects to this. It can be imagined that men may get higher carbon allowances because the work they do is so often defined as more important. There is some possibility that women might become valued because ways of doing femininity might be more 'green'. The latter falls prey to old assumptions that women are somehow closer to nature. In fact, the relations between the social and natural are beginning to be revisited, partly because sociologists are trying to come to terms with the social consequences of adverse human impacts on the environment (Inglis *et al.* 2005). Nothing of substance has yet been said about how a climate-changed future might affect gender. If gender *differences* are reinforced then it might be thought likely that gender inequalities will continue.

Urry's two scenarios may not be the only possible outcomes of global climate change, and whatever those outcomes they might accentuate current inequalities or possibly shift privilege to new groups (Lever-Tracy 2008). Visions of a future within the restrictions of a changed climate suggest that the discourses of progress that defined the nineteenth and twentieth centuries may be replaced by notions of regress. There is the possibility that it may already be more difficult to summarize complex patterns of social change as either an improvement on, or worse than, the past. This may especially be the case in relation to gender. The question regarding the future of gender is not so much whether gender relations will be better or worse, but how they will be characterized. It is possible that gender may cease to be a significant social category.

SUMMARY

What I wish to indicate in this chapter is that there is nothing inevitable about the future of gender. It is tempting to feel overwhelmed by the possibilities that could arise from current complexity and to think that there will always be inequalities between women and men in some form. However, it is possible to imagine that 'men' and 'women' may not exist in the way we now understand those categories. What kind of categories of people might become important is almost impossible to predict. Yet people do predict and the resulting visions of the gendered future are a mixture of fancy and a collage shaped from the materials of today. By understanding what is happening now and how things have changed and are changing, sociologists should be well placed to make educated guesses about what the future may bring. Nevertheless, they have often shied away from visions of the future, perhaps aware of the mistakes of even great minds who have tried. Literary visions have been freer from concerns about veracitude and those with some political allegiance to feminism have provided inspiring visions of alternative possibilities for how gender might be organized. There are scholars as well as novel writers who are considering the future of gender. Some wonder whether, rather than a focus on gender, a future distinction might be made between those more authentically human and those more machine in a world of cyborgs. This raises questions about which group will have the greater status. Or the queering of gender might make flexible expressions of desire more important than sexed bodies. It is possible that 'women' will continue to describe a group who share disadvantages imposed on them because of how biological reproduction is organized in ways that exclude them from other social spheres. Periodically, traditional ideas about their place as emotional experts best fitted to be the nurturers of men and children may re-gain force. Whatever the future holds, everyday life will bear some resemblance to now and also be different. Changes relating to gender are certain because the everyday lives of women and men are not pre-programmed into their genes but shaped by social conditions and ideas.

CONCLUSION: GENDER, EVERYDAY LIFE AND DEGENDERING

In sociologically imagining the state of gender in everyday life I have packaged it up around themes that seem important: gendered embodiment, the learning and doing of gender, gender as relation(ships), resisting gender and future gender. In this Conclusion I want to draw together insights parcelled out in each chapter to give an overview of gender that is historical, comparative and critical. I do this so that some thought can be given to where thinking about gender might go next. The last major rethink of gender was by Judith Butler, whose first book on the topic appeared in 1990. This changed the way gender was thought about and I want to consider whether there might be any other revolutions in store. It would be nice to imagine that this Conclusion might contain such a revolution, but I have more humble hopes. I just hope that these last pages might leave you with a sense of why it is important to reflect on how gender is done in everyday life, how sociology can help with this, and to explore the possibility that gender could be done differently or even not at all.

HISTORY OF GENDER: LEARNING FROM THE PAST

Looking back at how women's and men's lives have changed is a crucial element in seeing how we are not simply determined by our biology. Bodies play a part in how we live and form the basis on which social divisions such as gender operate. However, bodies are not just hunks of indisputable flesh but are interpreted in changing ways. There have been different ways of thinking about human bodies and in the past women's and men's bodies were seen as more similar than they are now.

If gender is not simply programmed into our anatomy, then there are bound to be variations in how women and men act. There are patterns to these variations over time and Chapter 2 documented some of the changing ways in which femininity and masculinity have been done. Social expectations about 'ladylike' or 'manly' behaviour do shift, as you will know from sometimes hearing older folk exclaim about how what youngsters are doing or wearing would not have been acceptable 'in their day'. Sociologists think about the patterns around gender in terms of large processes that are going on within particular societies and how they have brought us to where we are today. They may attend to the economic shifts that have taken place, for example. The emergence of a capitalist economy based on manufacturing in eighteenth-century Britain brought urbanization, and instigated a separation between home and work that had profound effects on individual men's and women's lives. Major changes in ideas and the meanings attached to gender have been related to changes in the way society is organized around gender. There is a general perception that inequalities between women and men are no longer acceptable, but the notion that women should act differently from men is still a powerful one.

Gender is not done in isolation, it is done in relation to others. There have been crucial changes in how these relations operate, both in the wider society and within intimate relationships. Up until the mid-twentieth century women's lives tended to revolve around their families. As more women entered the workforce, they were subject to less control from fathers and husbands, but more control from employers and other powerful figures within the public world. These figures were usually men within a society that continues, despite many advances for women, to be male dominated. However, family life has also changed considerably, as have the kinds of family that exist. Couples are likely to cohabit before marrying, if they marry at all. People are having children later. Same-sex couples are receiving some recognition. Nevertheless, despite some shifts away from traditional types of intimate relationship, where women and men live together, there are still struggles over who does the washing-up, as well as more serious conflicts.

Although the way society is organized restricts people in gendered ways, there have always been spaces for doing things differently. This book shows how women have historically faced greater restrictions within a male-dominated society. However, there have always been women who have protested against the limitations of their lives, and the chapter on resistance began by examining some of the early writings advocating more freedom for women. Later, mass movements emerged that championed women's rights, and brought significant changes such as the right to vote, to education and, later, to equal pay. Gradually there have been shifts in how gender in everyday life works.

Previous attempts to imagine future gender shifts have often failed to think beyond differences between women and men as natural and unchangeable. Early sociologists, with notable exceptions such as Harriet Martineau, tended to think little about differences between women and men and, when they did imagine any change, it was that women would become more like men by entering the workforce (Marx and Weber), or women would specialize in the caring work at home within the family (Durkheim). More radical visions could be found in science fiction, but these, too, often struggled at some point to escape the idea that women and men just were different. Only in rare cases has the future been imagined as degendered, and some discussion of comparisons might help reveal why.

COMPARATIVE APPROACHES TO GENDER

It does seem to be the case that most cultures and most social groups do make gender distinctions, but they do not make them in the same way. Even within lesbian culture, for example, some women are labelled 'butch' and some 'femme'. However, there are groups who are not particularly interested in distinguishing feminine from masculine. One classic example comes from anthropologist Margaret Mead's comparative study of gender in three different tribes in New Guinea. She noted that the Arapesh of New Guinea regarded both women and men as 'inherently gentle, responsive and co-operative', and that both women and men of the tribe took responsibility for childcare (Mead 1963/1935: 134). I have given other examples, within Chapter 1, about different cultures where rather than just feminine versus masculine there are one or two 'in between' genders. And of course there is considerable variation in the kinds of actions considered feminine or masculine by different groups, both across and within cultures.

One of the major variations in doing gender occurs around class. A society's dominant ideas about femininity and masculinity are usually the ideas of the dominant class. These ideals of femininity promote a ladylike delicacy, while the most rewarded styles of masculinity are besuited and physically and emotionally restrained. Although working-class women and men may take a certain pride in not being pretentious, they may also often feel put down or inadequate when measured against standards of respectability not of their own inventing. There are likely to be real effects involved in the lack of respect from which the working classes often suffer. Getting a decent education, decent job and indeed a decent life may remain a struggle for working-class women and men when they are constantly judged to be tarts and thugs. As this suggests, the doing of gender is not achieved by individuals in isolation.

Gender is a relation. What it means and how it is done always relies on other people and other meanings and doings. Gender relations are organized at a social level such that women and men are typically thought suited for, and channelled into, different types of task. While women have made inroads into many formerly male occupations, one of the areas in which gendered divisions of labour have changed only very slowly is the home. The gap between the amount of housework women and men do may have closed a little, but it still remains substantial. That women continue to do the vast majority of the cleaning and caring work within intimate relationships is one indication of the persistence of gender inequalities. It is difficult for women to juggle work and family. This may be one reason why less traditional types of relationship are gaining ground. Non-conventional relationships, from same-sex families to living apart together, may provide better opportunities for doing gender in more equal ways.

Intimate relationships are not the only realm in which change occurs, and specific political attempts to bring changes to gender relations have come not only from women's movements, but a politics of masculinity. Comparing this politics to the success of women's movements can help explain how positive change can occur. In examining the variety of ways in which masculinity can be resisted in everyday life it is important to note that not all men are in positions of power. However, notions that men are somehow *meant* to have power and privilege remain persistent. Sometimes men who have been marginalized try to regain some sense of control by restricting the lives of women. Others turn to self-destruction, trying to prove their toughness by constantly engaging in danger and violence. In the case of pro-feminist men who recognize that society tends to privilege men, real possibilities arise for doing gender relations in more equal ways. This is because they focus not on trying to feel better about themselves, but on achieving wider social changes that would bring greater equality.

What form social changes affecting gender might take in the future is the subject of considerable debate. They deserve a critical evaluation more easily executed if we take stock of the major perspectives on gender and everyday life.

THINKING CRITICALLY

There is a wide variety of sociological and feminist approaches to gender and I cover only some in this book, focusing on those that deal most with the everyday aspects of gender. I have dealt with how the approaches covered critically address the key issues relevant to a sociological understanding of gender. These I see as follows:

- Differences between women and men are socially constructed, not biologically determined.
- Gender is learned and practised every day in relation to norms/rules/scripts.
- It is useful to consider whether we do gender, it is done to us, or produces us.
- There continue to be gender inequalities and social problems around gender.
- Processes of individualization and globalization foster new fashionings of gendered selves.
- Social and technological change continues to affect gender, and the future of gender may see continuities or breaks with the past.
- The most radical change would be for gender to disappear.

This is my synthesis of different ideas about gender, and drawing existing ideas together in such a way is a critical enterprise. Each chapter has taken one of these issues as the substance of its critical section, but by piecing back together those parts a bigger picture can emerge. This is not a grand scheme that will finally explain everything about gender, but by doing this I hope to show you how to think critically and to clarify how sociology helps understand gender in everyday life.

The first bullet point states what I regard as the most crucial insight sociologists have to offer about gender and everyday life: that gender is socially constructed. While acknowledging that bodies are crucial – after all, we spend much of each day attending to bodily needs – it is important to see human bodies as always embedded within social life. How we attend to our bodily needs and what we think bodies mean are socially constructed. Thinking this way helps me have hope. There is something depressing and even paralyzing about the idea that we are always driven by our genes or our hormones. Not even geneticists really believe that. Possessing a gene for alcoholism does not mean I will inevitably become an alcoholic. I may have a slightly higher risk than someone without that gene, but whether I turn to alcoholism or not depends on the changing social environment in which I live out my life. Some people appear to find a belief in 'natural' differences between women and men reassuring. I can understand that, because those differences can be enormously frustrating, and if they are 'natural' then there is a sense that they cannot be helped and therefore we might be able to move towards a sense of calm acceptance. The alternative – believing that those differences are fundamentally socially created – implies that we all have much more responsibility for dealing with those frustrations. But sociologists are not suggesting that it is up to individuals to construct gender differently. It is not that easy, because no one sat down round a table and said: 'Let's organize society along gendered lines and here's how we're going to do it.' Society *is* heavily organized along gendered lines, from games at school to jobs to who cleans the toilet. However, the social construction of gender is full of contradictions, disagreements and confusions. How am I supposed to do femininity? I could doll myself up and wear high heels but someone is likely to think I look vulgar. The point is that if gender is socially constructed and not everyone knows or agrees exactly what it is, there are spaces and possibilities. This doesn't have to be how it is – gender is open to change, it could be made less frustrating.

There are already, as we have seen, a range of ways in which gender is learned and practised in everyday life. There are norms and rules and scripts that set out the most socially favoured ways of doing gender. These shift and change throughout history and from one culture or social group to another. When I was young doctors were rarely women, now they often are. Using moisturizer or taking an interest in clothes does not now automatically lead to a man being identified as gay. It is not a case of 'anything goes' – there are dominant patterns to how we learn femininity and masculinity, and early socialization is powerful in making girls girly and boys boyish. This does not mean that it is all mummy's fault. Parents do not live in a bubble with their children, and extended families, nurseries, schools, workplaces and the media are other sources of gender socialization. These communicate a range of sometimes conflicting ideas about how to do gender, so children do have a somewhat active part in learning gender in that there are choices to be made between the possibilities available. However, symbolic interactionists go further in that they suggest that gender is something we constantly have to learn and practise throughout our lives. We are always working at trying to get it 'right'. We continue to learn and do gender, according to this perspective, in interaction with others. However, there are those who suggest that saying that we 'do' gender puts too much emphasis on individuals' ability to choose.

The third bullet point touches on an ongoing debate within sociology about the extent to which our lives are governed by the way society is organized (structure) and how much power we have to choose (agency). Symbolic interactionists may veer a little towards the agency side of this debate, but they do think that there are structures, even at the level of everyday life, that constrain how gender is done. There are 'scripts' that set out 'normal' expectations about doing gender in various social situations from workplaces to parties to intimate relationships. People can play out those scripts with some variations. For example, almost all the knowledge I had of how to lecture sociology when I became an academic, was from being lectured to by men. There were few women academics when I was studying. Doing lecturing was therefore muddled up with doing masculinity for me. It took me a while to figure out how to be a woman lecturer, and I think I still sometimes rub my chin thoughtfully as though I have a beard. And even if I have varied the script for that situation, sometimes others 'do' my gender for me in those interactions, in ways I may not like. For example, when I was younger I once got some obscene comments about my breasts on student evaluation forms. I thought I was being feminine yet scholarly, but a few (male?) students were doing my gender by sexually objectifying me. Maybe this made it less threatening for them dealing with a young woman lecturer, when most gender scripts encourage women to play down their intelligence and play up men's. The point is that there are limits to freely doing gender however we wish because gender is also done to us by others. Sitting alone, thinking about nothing in particular it may be possible that we sometimes 'forget' about our gender. However, in interaction we are liable to be reminded. Butler argues that gender fundamentally creates individuals according to current norms. It is not that gender is an aspect of who we are, but that gender is *the* main system through which social beings are produced. Gender is not simply done by us or to us, but it does us. Yet it never does us completely. The norms can only be approximated, so each gendered individual in imitating the norms does so slightly differently. Gender is not an actual property that individual women share and men have in common, but an illusion or a masquerade around which only certain ways of being human are possible. Every human being is understood in gendered terms, but almost always they are somehow not feminine enough or too masculine, and so on. This means that what it means to be gendered is never fixed, that we can never get it 'right'.

All that is certain is that being feminine means not being masculine, and vice versa. However, in our everyday lives we are all aware that women can sometimes be considered masculine and men feminine. This troubles the gender system and, if the boundary between feminine and masculine can be blurred, then that system can become less constraining.

As it stands, the binary opposition between feminine and masculine creates a gender system that perpetuates inequalities. The male-dominated societies in which we live tend to privilege men and disadvantage women. The problem is that 'feminine' and 'masculine' are not considered equal opposites. Whatever is masculine at various different times and in different places is rated superior to what is feminine. Maleness and masculinity tend to carry with them greater social rewards: more money, more power, more prestige. Not all men share equally in these rewards, and not all women are equally excluded. There are other inequalities in the dividing up of social goodies around class, race/ethnicity, age, disability and sexuality. However, generally speaking, men are likely to benefit more than women from the current way in which society is organized. Some men might recognize this and feel guilty, some women may believe that their proper place is in the home. Whether people are happy or unhappy with the way society works they are still affected by it. The men who feel guilty cannot instantly avoid all the privileges they receive by being men. Women who want to stay at home and care for their families might find that difficult in times where both partners are under pressure to work in order to pay a mortgage and provide the things their kids want. Individuals are still influenced by social norms, even if their experiences differ from the norm. My experience of close relationships with men has been overwhelmingly one of kindness and gentleness from them, but I am well aware, from speaking to other women and from looking at the statistics, that this is not the case for large numbers of women who are subject to violence from the men in their lives. But I cannot escape that violence completely and it could be argued that the obscene comments those students made about me are in a small way an act of violence designed to punish me for straying into masculine territory. As C. Wright Mills said, we need to sort out what are private troubles from what are public issues. And, for sociologists, it is important to think about social problems. These are public issues that negatively affect large groups of people. For example, if one or two men are being occasionally slapped by their wives that is not to be condoned, but still qualifies as a private trouble. On the other hand, if huge numbers of women are being severely beaten and killed by men because they are somehow not doing what their man thinks a good woman should, that is a public issue. This violence against women is a social problem and one of the worst things that results from gender inequalities.

There are always new social problems arising and gendering within everyday life is something individuals often resist as they are swept up by processes of individualization and globalization. These processes can be overwhelming as tradition becomes a less and less automatic arbiter of action. People face constant choices about how to live their lives, and yet some people have far fewer resources and far less power to call on in overcoming obstacles. Global connections, both economic and environmental, are almost impossible to ignore, but they work better for some than for others. For most women individualization has been limited by caring obligations, or at least by the way in which paid work does not easily accommodate care work done at home. Women and men with more resources and power are still affected by individualization and globalization but have more options in responding to or alleviating that constraint. Many appear to be turning to self-fashioning as a response. These self-fashionings are highly gendered, with women usually focusing on looking more feminine according to dominant ideals that emphasize slender, respectable whiteness. Men, to a lesser degree and in different ways, are also subject to social pressures that require them to display toned and controlled bodies as a signal of their ability to take charge. Through diet and dress and exercise people try to discipline their bodies, but they may sometimes do this in ways that resist rather than accommodate gender norms. These forms of resistance may blur gender boundaries, but emphasis on the self rather than on wider social structures is unlikely to really challenge how gender relations perpetuate inequalities.

As society changes and humans respond to and create change – for example, through the creation of new technologies – gender will continue to shift. In the 1990s there was considerable interest in the impact of bio-technologies that made humans part machine. These cyborg technologies can be used to reinforce sex/gender differences – for example, via breast implants or bra technology. However, the same and other technologies may blur gender boundaries as transvestites wear special bras or individuals undergo sex-change operations. Whether such technology brings positive change is debated and some fear that gender may be reinforced in restrictive ways, or that embodied femininity may be threatened with disappearance. It could be that blurring means masculinization, rather than real change. And indeed other debates question the extent to which tradition has ceased to guide people's lives, many arguing that in many areas a retraditionalization of gender has occurred that has pushed many women back into restrictive feminine roles, rather than bringing positive change.

I have suggested that the most radical change would be for gender to disappear, but only if that meant an end to gender inequalities. Some queer theorists propose this, or at least that gender can become much more fluid. What is difficult to imagine is a world without any gender categories at all. But if this book tells us anything it tells us that gender is a system that is socially created and other ways of organizing the social world are possible. Have another think about your day and how it would differ if your sex/gender was no longer an issue, no more an issue than whether you have brown eyes rather than blue eyes, or big ears instead of little ears. Would everything have to be thought of differently, from pyjamas, to washing and dressing, to breakfast, to work, to how the evening meal was prepared and by whom, to how to relate to any children and what stories they were read at bedtime? Most people do not think much about how gender may creep into these everyday spaces. Yet even trivial matters like gender-neutral pyjamas are difficult to conjure up in the mind: no Spider-Man, no flowers or lace. And the shape is uncertain – they could be trousers and tops or like nightshirts. The toiletries in the bathroom would have to be redesigned. Gone would be the functional, subdued packaging of men's products, versus the colour (especially pink) and the flowers and other 'feminine touches' sprinkled on anything for women. Would ordinary soap be safely degendered or is Imperial Leather 'man's soap'? Obviously clothes could be an issue. Trousers have been adopted by women, and jeans can be pretty androgynous, but there are differences in the way trousers are worn by women and men that would disappear. And maybe everyone would sometimes wear some kind of skirt or dress. Bras might be considered ancient and barbaric devices, which is largely how we view corsets now. People with breasts (and some men have breasts) would no more think of wearing a bra than people with big ears feel they should bandage them to their head. Then two (or more?) people with no bras, in some kind of skirts might sit down to breakfast together without feeling the need to have either a delicate portion of fruit or a manly serving of bacon and eggs. Some in-between consumption of toast may occur (or fruit some days, bacon and eggs others) before going off to work at jobs divided not according to a gendered division of labour, but according to each person's merits. Construction sites would contain people with a wider variety of bodies than they do now, although all those bodies would be strong. Less strong people with different skills might do clerical or service work. People in power, at the top of companies and in charge of countries, would be a better mix of types of people than at present, as would those professionally caring for others in hospitals, childcare facilities and nursing homes. There would be different ways of caring for children that did not necessarily entail one person having to stay at home. Maybe workplaces would all have a crèche so that parents could visit children at lunchtime or pop in for morning tea. If there are two (or more?) parents involved with the kids, the kids might go to one parent's workplace one week and another's the next, and so on. Or paid parental leave would be available for any parent if they wanted to stay at home with the kids. But home and work might not even be separated in the way they are now, so other things might be possible. Kids not tied in to having to try to be boyish or girlish might have some unexpected stories to tell us in the evenings.

The idea of a social world without gender may seem a little like some weird fairy story for feminist bedtimes, but we need to imagine it. Imagining and debating about creating different ways of living is crucial given the major challenges the world currently faces. There are profoundly gendered aspects to global inequalities, environmental degradation, and burgeoning violent conflict in the form of wars and terrorism. Those of us in what seem safer countries may not feel that these are part of our everyday life, yet they do not only appear on our televisions. For example, I currently live in Australia. Nearly all the clothes on sale here are made in China because workers there are much cheaper to employ. I get cheap clothes because many women in China are working long hours in poor conditions (Klein 2002/2000). And I live in the driest state: South Australia. Global warming is not something just threatening Caribou populations in the Arctic on which some Inuit peoples are highly dependent. It is not just something bringing famine and war to Darfur, or flooding to Bangladesh, both of which are creating huge numbers of refugees. It is also making water scarce and food expensive in Australia. This is presently manageable for a more privileged nation and for more privileged women such as myself, but makes everyday life more of a struggle for Australian men and women on low incomes, especially single mothers with children to care for. Changing the world is not as simple as giving up 'macho' four-wheel drives (often beloved by wealthier mothers with small children) or looking at who is clocking up air miles doing business around the world. It is not that men are naturally suited to sitting on aeroplanes, nor to killing each other while women make porridge and babies. We don't have to live this way. Sociological criticism should bewail the terrible state of the world, but it should also imagine, debate and hope for better.

REFERENCES

Abercrombie, N., Hill, S. and Turner, B.S. (1984) *Dictionary of Sociology*, London: Penguin.

Adkins, L. (2000) 'Objects of innovation: post-occupational reflexivity and re-traditionalisations of gender', in S. Ahmed, J. Kilby, C. Lury, M. McNeil and B. Skeggs (eds) *Transformations: Thinking Though Feminism*, London: Routledge.

Afshar, H. (1997) 'Women and work in Iran', *Political Studies*, 45 (4), 755–767.

Allen, L. (2003) 'Girls want sex, boys want love: resisting dominant discourses of (hetero) sexuality', *Sexualities*, 6 (2), 215–236.

Arendell, T. (2000) 'Conceiving and investigating motherhood: the decade's scholarship', *Journal of Marriage and Family*, 62 (4), 1192–1207.

Aries, P. (1962) *Centuries of Childhood: a Social History of Family Life* (transl. Robert Baldick), New York: Vintage Books/Random House; London: Jonathan Cape.

Atwood, M. (1986) *The Handmaid's Tale*, London: Jonathan Cape.

Australian Bureau of Statistics (2007) 'Mother Day 2007 and National Families Week: ABS (media release)', 11 May, available at http://www.abs.gov.au.

Australian Institute of Health and Welfare (2005) 'Female SAAP clients escaping domestic and family violence 2003–04', *Australian Institute of Health and Welfare Bulletin*, 30, 1–27.

Balsamo, A. (2003) 'Forms of technological embodiment: reading the body in contemporary culture', in A. Blaikie, M. Hepworth, M. Holmes, A. Howson, D. Inglis and S. Sartain (eds) *The Body: Critical Concepts in Sociology* (Volume V), London: Routledge, 53–75.

Bauman, Z. (1998) *Globalization: The Human Consequences*, New York: Columbia University Press.

Baxter, J. (2005) 'To marry or not to marry: marital status and the household division of labor', *Journal of Family Issues*, 26 (3), 300–321.

Beasley, C. (2005) *Gender and Sexuality: Critical Theories, Critical Thinkers*, London: Sage.

Beck, U. and Beck-Gernsheim, E. (1995) *The Normal Chaos of Love*, Cambridge, UK: Polity Press.

Beck, U. and Beck-Gernsheim, E. (2002) *Individualization: Institutionalized Individualism and its Social and Political Consequences*, London: Sage.

Benhabib, S. (1987) 'The generalized and the concrete other: the Kohlberg-Gilligan controversy and feminist theory', in S. Benhabib and D. Cornell (eds) *Feminism as Critique: On the Politics of Gender*, Minneapolis, MN: University of Minnesota Press.

Berger, P. (1966/1963) *Invitation to Sociology: A Humanistic Perspective*, Harmondsworth: Penguin.

Bernard, J. (1981) *The Female World*, New York: Free Press.

Besnier, N. (1994) 'Polynesian gender liminality through time and space', in G. Herdt (ed.) *Third Sex, Third Gender: Beyond Sexual Dimorphism in Culture and History*, New York: Zone, 285–328.

Betterton, R. (1987) 'Introduction: feminism, femininity and representation', in R. Betterton, *Looking On: Images of Femininity in the Visual Arts and Media*, London: Routledge.

Black, P. (2004) *The Beauty Industry: Gender, Culture, Pleasure*, London: Routledge.

Bly, R. (1990) *Iron John: A Book About Men*, Reading, MA: Addison-Wesley.

Boje, T.P. (2007) 'Welfare and work. The gendered organisation of work and care in different European countries', *European Review*, 15 (3), 373–395.

Bordo, S. (1989) 'The body and the reproduction of femininity: a feminist appropriation of Foucault', in S. Bordo and A.S. Jagger (eds) *Gender/Body/Knowledge*, New Brunswick, NJ: Rutgers University Press.

Bordo, S. (1993) *Unbearable Weight: Feminism, Western Culture and the Body*, Berkeley, CA: University of California Press.

Boushey, H. (2007) 'Perspectives on work/family balance and the Federal Equal Employment Opportunity Laws', Meeting of 17 April, US Equal Employment Opportunity Commission, available at http://www.eeoc.gov/abouteeoc/meetings/4–17–07/boushey.html.

Brace-Govan, J. (2004) 'Weighty matters: control of women's access to physical strength', *The Sociological Review*, 52 (4), 503–531.

Braidotti, R. (2001) *Metamorphoses: Towards a Materialist Theory of Becoming*, Cambridge: Polity.

Brannen, J. and Collard, J. (1982) *Marriages in Trouble: The Process of Seeking Help*, London: Tavistock.

Brook, H. (2007) *Conjugal Rites: Marriage and Marriage-like Relationships before the Law*, New York: Palgrave Macmillan.

Brookes, B. (1991) 'Annemarie anon', in C. Macdonald, M. Penfold and B. Williams (eds) *The Book of New Zealand Women: Ko Kui Ma Te Kaupapa*, Wellington: Bridget Williams Books, 14–15.

Butler, J. (1990) *Gender Trouble: Feminism and the Subversion of Identity*, London: Routledge.

Butler, J. (1992) 'Contingent foundations: feminism and the question of "postmodernism" ', in J. Butler and J. Scott (eds) *Feminists Theorize the Political*, New York: Routledge.

Butler, J. (1993) *Bodies That Matter: On the Discursive Limits of 'Sex'*, London: Routledge.

Butler, J. (2004) *Undoing Gender*, New York and London: Routledge.

Byne, W., Tobet, S., Mattiace, L.A., Lasco, M.S., Kemether, E., Edgar, M.A., Morgello, S., Buchsbaum, M.S. and Jones, L.B. (2001) 'The interstitial nuclei of the human anterior hypothalamus: an investigation of variation with sex, sexual orientation, and HIV status', *Hormones and Behavior*, 40 (2), 86–92.

Cancian, F.M. (1986) 'The feminization of love', *Signs*, 11, 692–709.

Catalyst (2007) 'Women gain board committee chairs in the Fortune 500', available at http://www.catalyst.org/.

Cavanagh, K., Dobash, R.E., Dobash, R.P. and Lewis, R. (2001) ' "Remedial work": men's strategic responses to their violence against intimate female partners', *Sociology*, 35 (3), 695–714.

Charles, M. and Grusky, D.B. (2004) *Occupational Ghettos: The Worldwide Segregation of Women and Men*, Palo Alto, CA: Stanford University Press.

Comte, A. (1974/1853) *The Positive Philosophy of Auguste Comte* (transl. and condensed by Harriet Martineau), New York: AMS Press.

Connell, R.W. (1995) *Masculinities*, Cambridge: Polity Press.

Connell, R.W. (2002) *Gender*, Cambridge: Polity.

Connell, R.W. (2005) 'Globalization, imperialism and masculinities', in M.S. Kimmel, J. Hearn and R.W. Connell (eds) *Handbook of Studies on Men and Masculinities*, Thousand Oaks, CA: Sage, 71–89.

Connell, R.W., Ashden, D., Kessler, S. and Dowsett, G. (1982) *Making the Difference: Schools, Families and Social Divisions*, Sydney: Allen & Unwin.

Crompton, R. and Lyonette, C. (2006) 'Work–life "balance" in Europe', *Acta Sociologica*, 49 (4), 379–393.

Davidoff, L. and Hall, C. (1987) *Family Fortunes: Men and Women of the English Middle Class, 1780–1850*, Chicago, IL: University of Chicago Press.

Davies, B. (1993) *Shards of Glass: Children Reading and Writing Beyond Gendered Identities*, St Leonards, NSW: Allen & Unwin.

Davis, K. (1995) *Reshaping the Female Body: The Dilemma of Cosmetic Surgery*, London and New York: Routledge.

Delamont, S. (1978) 'The domestic ideology and women's education', in S.

Delamont and L. Duffin (eds) *The Nineteenth Century Woman*, London: Croom Helm, 134–187.

Delamont, S. (1990) *A Woman's Place in Education: Historical and Sociological Perspectives on Gender in Education*, Aldershot: Avebury.

Dobash, R.E. and Dobash, R. (1979) *Violence Against Wives: A Case Against the Patriarchy*, New York: Free Press.

Duggan, L. and Hunter, N.D. (2006) *Sex Wars: Sexual Dissent and Political Culture*, London: Routledge.

Duncombe, J. and Marsden, D. (1993) 'Love and intimacy: the gender division of emotion and emotion work, a neglected aspect of sociological discussion of heterosexual relationships', *Sociology*, 27 (2), 221–241.

Duncombe, J. and Marsden, D. (1995) ' "Workaholics" and "whingeing women": theorising intimacy and emotion work – the last frontier of gender inequality?', *Sociological Review*, 43 (1), 150–169.

Durkheim, E. (1933/1893) *The Division of Labor in Society* (transl. George Smith), New York: Collier Macmillan/The Free Press.

Dworkin, A. (1981) *Pornography: Men Possessing Women*, London: Women's Press.

Edwards, J. and McKie, L. (1996) 'Women's public toilets: a serious issue for the body politic', *European Journal of Women's Studies*, 3 (3), 215–232.

Elias, N. (2000/1939) *The Civilizing Process: Sociogenetic and Psychogenetic Investigations*, Oxford: Blackwell.

Engels, F. (1969/1845) *The Condition of the Working Class in England*, London: Panther.

Engels, F. (1985/1884) *The Origin of the Family, Private Property and the State*, Harmondsworth: Penguin.

Erickson, R.J. (2005) 'Why emotion work matters: sex, gender, and the division of household labor', *Journal of Marriage and Family*, 67 (2), 337–351.

Eriksen, W., Bruusgaard, D. and Knardahl, S. (2004) 'Work factors as predictors of intense or disabling low back pain; a prospective study of nurses' aides', *Occupational and Environmental Medicine*, 61, 398–404.

Evans, J. (1995) *Feminist Theory Today: An Introduction to Second-Wave Feminism*, Edinburgh: Edinburgh University Press.

Evans, R. (1977) *The Feminists: Women's Emancipation Movements in Europe, America and Australasia 1840–1920*, London and Totowa NJ: Croom Helm and Barnes & Noble.

Faludi, S. (1991) *Backlash: The Undeclared War Against Women*, London: Chatto & Windus.

Faludi, S. (1999) *Stiffed: The Betrayal of the Modern Man*, London: Chatto & Windus.

Fausto-Sterling, A. (2000) *Sexing the Body: Gender Politics and the Construction of Sexuality*, New York: Basic Books.

Fausto-Sterling, A. (2002) 'The five sexes, revisited', *Sciences*, 40, 18–23.

Featherstone, M. (1991) 'The body in consumer culture', in M. Featherstone,

M. Hepworth and B. Turner (eds) *The Body: Social Process and Cultural Theory*, London: Sage.

Finkelstein, J. (1991) *The Fashioned Self*, Cambridge: Polity.

Finkelstein, J. (1996) *After a Fashion*, Carlton, Vic.: Melbourne University Press.

Foucault, M. (1980) *Power/Knowledge: Selected Interviews and Other Writings 1972–1977* (ed. Colin Gordon), London: Harvester Wheatsheaf.

Foucault, M. (1990) *The History of Sexuality, 1. An Introduction* (transl. Robert Hurley), Harmondsworth: Penguin.

Freidan, B. (1965) *The Feminine Mystique*, New York: Norton.

Gamman, L. and Marshment, M. (1988) *The Female Gaze: Women as Viewers of Popular Culture*, London: The Women's Press.

Garfinkel, H. (1967) *Studies in Ethnomethodology*, Englewood Cliffs, NJ: Prentice Hall.

Gauntlett, D. (2002) *Media, Gender, and Identity: An Introduction*, London and New York: Routledge.

Gearhart, S.M. (1985) *The Wanderground: Stories of the Hill Women*, London: Women's Press.

Giddens, A. (1986) *Sociology: A Brief but Critical Introduction*, Basingstoke: Macmillan.

Giddens, A. (1990) *The Consequences of Modernity*. Stanford, CA: Stanford University Press.

Giddens, A. (1992) *The Transformation of Intimacy: Sexuality, Love and Eroticism in Modern Societies*, Stanford, CA: Stanford University Press.

Gimlin, D.L. (2001) *Body Work: Beauty and Self Image in American Culture*, Berkeley, CA: University of California Press.

Gjerdingen, D.K. and Center, B.A. (2005) 'First-time parents' postpartum changes in employment, childcare, and housework responsibilities', *Social Science Research*, 34 (1), 103–116.

Goffman, E. (1979) *Gender Advertisements*, Basingstoke: Macmillan.

Goffman, E. (1987/1959) *The Presentation of Self in Everyday Life*, Harmondsworth: Penguin.

Goldin, C. & Katz, L.F. (2002) 'The power of the pill: oral contraceptives and women's career and marriage decisions', *Journal of Political Economy*, 110 (4), 730–770.

Green, B. (1997) *Spectacular Confessions: Autobiography, Performative Activism and the Sites of Suffrage 1905–1938*, New York: St Martin's Press.

Haier, R.J., Jung, R.E., Yeo, R.A., Head, K. and Alkire, M.T. (2005) 'The neuro-anatomy of general intelligence: sex matters', *NeuroImage*, 25, 320–327.

Haraway, D. (1985) 'A manifesto for cyborgs: science, technology, and socialist feminism in the 1980s', *Socialist Review*, 80, 65–108.

Haraway, D. (1997) *Modest_Witness@Second_Millenium.FemaleMan©_Meets_OncoMouse™: Feminism and Technoscience*, New York and London: Routledge.

Hargreaves, J. (1997) 'Women's boxing and related activities: introducing images and meanings', *Body and Society*, 3 (4), 33–49.

Hartmann, H. (1976) 'Capitalism, patriarchy and job segregation by sex', *Signs*, 1 (3), 137–168.

Hartmann, H. (1981) 'The unhappy marriage of Marxism and feminism: towards a more progressive union', in L. Sargent (ed.) *Women and Revolution: The Unhappy Marriage of Marxism and Feminism*, London: Pluto Press.

Harvey, K. (2005) 'The history of masculinity, circa 1650–1800', *Journal of British Studies*, 44 (2), 296–311.

Herdt, G. (ed.) (1994) *Third Sex, Third Gender: Beyond Sexual Dimorphism in Culture and History*, New York: Zone.

Hill, M.R. and Hoecker-Drysdale, S. (eds) (2001) *Harriet Martineau: Theoretical and Methodological Perspectives*, London: Routledge.

Hird, M. (2004) *Sex, Gender, and Science*, New York: Palgrave.

Hochschild, A.R. (with Anne Machung) (1989) *The Second Shift: Working Parents and the Revolution at Home*, New York: Viking Penguin.

Hochschild, A.R. and Ehrenreich, B. (2004) *Global Woman: Nannies, Maids, and Sex Workers in the New Economy*, London: Granta

Hoecker-Drysdale, S. (2003) 'Harriet Martineau and the Positivism of Auguste Comte', in M.R. Hill and S. Hoecker-Drysdale (eds) *Harriet Martineau: Theoretical and Methodological Perspectives*, New York and London: Routledge, 169–189.

Holmes, M. (1991) 'Recovering the satin couch: the "pioneer woman" and the "new woman", in New Zealand'. Unpublished master's thesis, University of York.

Holmes, M. (2000a) 'When is the personal political? The President's penis and other stories', *Sociology*, 34 (2), 305–321.

Holmes, M. (2000b) 'Second-wave feminism and the politics of relationships', *Women's Studies International Forum*, 23 (2), 235–246.

Holmes, M. (2004) 'An equal distance? Individualisation, gender and intimacy in distance relationships', *The Sociological Review*, 52 (2), 180–200.

Holmes, M. (2007a) 'The emotionalization of reflexivity', paper presented at The Australian Sociological Association, University of Auckland, 4–7 December.

Holmes, M. (2007b) *What is Gender? Sociological Approaches*, London: Sage.

Imam, A.M. (2000) 'The Muslim religious right ("fundamentalists") and sexuality', in P. Ilkkaracan (ed.) *Women and Sexuality in Muslim Societies*, Istanbul: Women for Women's Human Rights, Kafinin Haklari Projesi, 121–139.

Inglis, D., Bone, J. and Wilkie, R. (2005) 'Nature: perceiving life inside and outside social scientific boundaries', in D. Inglis, J. Bone and R. Wilkie (eds) *Nature: Critical Concepts in the Social Sciences*, London: Routledge.

Inter-parliamentary Union (IPU) (2007) 'Women in national parliaments', situation as of 31 October 2007, accessed January 2008 at http://www.ipu.org/english/home.htm.

Intersex Society of North America (2006) http://www.isna.org/.

Jackson, S. (1998) 'Feminist social theory', in S. Jackson and J. Jones (eds) *Contemporary Feminist Theories*, Edinburgh: Edinburgh University Press.

Jackson, S. and Scott, S. (1996) 'Sexual skirmishes and feminist factions: twenty-five years of debate on women and sexuality', in S. Jackson & S. Scott (eds) *Feminism and Sexuality: A Reader*, Edinburgh: Edinburgh University Press, 1–31.

Jeffreys, S. (1996) 'Heterosexuality and the desire for gender', in D. Richardson (ed.) *Theorising Heterosexuality: Telling it Straight*, Buckingham, UK, and Philadelphia, PA: Open University Press.

Jordan, J. (2001) *Josephine Butler*, London: John Murray.

Jordanova, L. (1989) *Sexual Visions: Images of Gender in Science and Medicine between the Eighteenth and Twentieth Centuries*, London: Harvester Wheatsheaf.

Kaiser, J. (1996) 'Scientists angle for answers', *Science*, 274, 1837–1838.

Kedgley, S. and Varnham, M. (eds) (1993) *Heading Nowhere in a Navy Blue Suit: Tales from the Feminist Revolution*, Wellington: Daphne Brasell Associates Press.

Kelly, L. (1997) 'A central issue: sexual violence and feminist theory', in S. Kemp and J. Squires (eds) *Feminisms*, Oxford: Oxford University Press.

Kessler, S.J. and McKenna, W. (1985/1978) *Gender: An Ethnomethodological Approach*, Chicago, IL: University of Chicago Press.

Kiernan, K. (2004) 'Cohabitation and divorce across nations and generations', in P.L. Chase-Lansdale, K. Kiernan and R. Friedman (eds) *Human Development across Lives and Generations: The Potential for Change*, New York: Cambridge University Press. Also available as CASEpaper 65 at http://sticerd.lse.ac.uk/Case.

Kimmel, J. (2006) 'Childcare, female employment and economic growth', *Community Development*, 37 (2), 71–85.

Kimmel, M. (2005) 'Globalization and its mal(e)contents: the gendered moral and political economy of terrorism', in M.S. Kimmel, J. Hearn and R.W. Connell (eds) *Handbook of Studies on Men and Masculinities*, Thousand Oaks, CA: Sage, 414–431.

King, D.S. (2006) 'Activists and emotional reflexivity: towards Touraine's subject as social movement', *Sociology*, 40 (5), 873–891.

King, D.S. (2007) 'Bounded emotionality', in S. Clegg and J. Bailey (eds) *International Encyclopaedia of Organization Studies*, London: Sage.

Klein, N. (2002/2000) *No Logo: No Space, No Choice, No Jobs*, New York: Picador.

Laqueur, T. (1990) *Making Sex: Body and Gender: From the Greeks to Freud*, Boston, MA: Harvard University Press.

Le Guin, U.K. (1969) *The Left Hand of Darkness*, New York: Ace Books.

Lemert, C. (2004) *Sociology After the Crisis* (2nd edn), Boulder, CO: Paradigm.

Lemert, C. and Elliott, A. (2006) *The New Individualism: The Emotional Costs of Globalization*, London: Routledge.

Le Vay, S. (1991) 'A difference in hypothalamic structure between homosexual and heterosexual men', *Science*, 253, 1034–1037.

Lever-Tracy, C. (2008) 'Global warming and sociology', *Current Sociology*, 56, forthcoming.

Levin, I. (2004) 'Living apart together: a new family form', *Current Sociology*, 52 (2), 223–240.

Lewis, J. (1984) *Women in England 1870–1950: Sexual Divisions and Social Change*, Sussex: Wheatsheaf.

Linden Research, Inc. (2007) 'What is Second Life? Meet people', available at http://secondlife.com/whatis/.

Lobban, G. (1975) 'Sex-roles in reading schemes', *Educational Review*, 27, 202–210.

Lowe, G.S. (1987) *Women in the Administrative Revolution: The Feminization of Clerical Work*, Toronto: University of Toronto Press.

McBride, I.D., Wyss, U.P., Cooke, T.D., Murphy, L., Phillips, J. and Olney, S.J. (1991) 'First metatarsophalangeal joint reaction forces during high-heel gait', *Foot and Ankle International*, 11 (5), 282–288.

McRobbie, A. (1991) *Feminism and Youth Culture: From Jackie to Just Seventeen*, Boston, MA: Unwin Hyman.

McShane, V. (1979) 'Wanted, a more political convention', *New Zealand Monthly Review*, 20 (211), 7–9.

Maguire, E.A., Gadian, E.S., Johnsrude, I.S., Good, C.D., Ashburner, J., Frackowiak, R.S. and Frith, C.D. (2000) 'Navigation-related structural change in the hippocampi of taxi drivers', *Proceedings of the National Academy of Sciences of the United States of America*, 97 (8), 4398–4403.

Mansfield, A. and McGinn, B. (1993) 'Pumping irony: the muscular and the feminine', in S. Scott and D. Morgan (eds) *Body Matters: Essays on the Sociology of the Body*, London: Falmer Press, 49–68.

Martineau, H. (1837) *Society in America*, London: Saunders & Otley, available via http://books.google.com.au/ (accessed January 2005).

Mead, M. (1963/1935) *Sex and Temperament in Three Primitive Societies*, New York: William Morrow.

Messner, M.A. (1997) *The Politics of Masculinities: Men in Movements*, Thousand Oaks, CA: Sage.

Meyerowitz, J. (2002) *How Sex Changed: A History of Transsexuality in the United States*, Cambridge, MA: Harvard University Press.

Millet, K. (1972/1970) *Sexual Politics*, London: Abacus.

Mills, C.W. (1956) *White Collar: The American Middle Classes*, New York: Galaxy/Oxford University Press.

Mills, C.W. (1959) *The Sociological Imagination*, Oxford: Oxford University Press.

Morgan, D. (1993) 'You too can have a body like mine: reflections on the male body and masculinities', in S. Scott and D. Morgan (eds) *Body Matters: Essays on the Sociology of the Body*, London; Falmer Press.

Morgan, S.P. and Taylor, M.G. (2006) 'Low fertility at the turn of the twenty-first century', *Annual Review of Sociology*, 32, 375–399.

Mulvey, L. (1975) 'Visual pleasure and narrative cinema', *Screen*, 16 (3), 6–18.

Nanda, S. (1994) 'Hijras: an alternative sex and gender role in India', in G. Herdt (ed.) *Third Sex, Third Gender: Beyond Sexual Dimorphism in Culture and History*, New York: Zone.

Nazroo, J. (1999) 'Uncovering gender differences in the use of marital violence: the effect of methodology', in G. Allan (ed.) *The Sociology of the Family: A Reader*, Oxford: Blackwell.

Nicholson, A. (2008) 'Choose to hug, not hit', *Family Court Review*, 46 (1), 11–36.

Oakley, A. (1972) *Sex, Gender and Society*, London: Temple Smith.

Oakley, A. (1974) *The Sociology of Housework*, London: Martin Robertson.

Office of National Statistics (2002) 'A summary of changes over time: marriage and cohabitation' and 'Chapter 5: Marriage and cohabitation', *Living in Britain 2001*, available at http://www.statistics.gov.uk/lib2001/Section3474.html and http://www.statistics.gov.uk/lib2001/Section3481.html.

Oudshoorn, N. (1994) *Beyond the Natural Body: An Archeology of Sex Hormones*, London: Routledge.

Pahl, R. and Spencer, L. (2004) 'Personal communities: not simply families of "fate" or "choice" ', *Current Sociology*, 52 (2), 199–222.

Parsons, T. and Bales, R.F. (1956) *Family Socialization and Interaction Process*, London: Routledge & Kegan Paul.

Pateman, C. (1988) *The Sexual Contract*, Stanford, CA: Stanford University Press.

Peplau, L.A. (1994) 'Men and women in love', in D.L. Sollie and L.S. Leslie (eds) *Gender, Families, and Close Relationships: Feminist Research Journeys*, Thousand Oaks, CA: Sage, 19–49.

Phillips, A. (1991) *Engendering Democracy*, Pennsylvania, PA: Pennsylvania University Press.

Pisan, C. de (2005) *The City of Ladies*, London: Penguin.

Plummer, D. (1999) *One of the Boys: Masculinity, Homophobia and Modern Manhood*, New York: Harrington Park Press.

Pocock, B. (2006) *The Labour Market Ate My Babies: Work, Children and a Sustainable Future*, Annandale, NSW: The Federation Press.

Pringle, R. and Winning, A. (1998) 'Building strategies: equal opportunity in the construction industry', *Gender, Work and Organization*, 5(4), 220–229.

Rendall, J. (1985) *Origins of Modern Feminism: Women in Britain, France and the United States, 1780–1860*, Basingstoke: Palgrave Macmillan.

Roscoe, W. (1994) 'How to become a berdache: toward a unified analysis of gender diversity', in G. Herdt (ed.) *Third Sex, Third Gender: Beyond Sexual Dimorphism in Culture and History*, New York: Zone, 329–372.

Roseneil, S. (2000) 'Queer frameworks and queer tendencies: towards an understanding of postmodern transformations of sexuality', *Sociological Research Online*, 5 (3), available at http://www.socresonline.org.uk/5/3/roseneil.html.

Roseneil, S. (2005) 'Living and loving beyond the boundaries of the heteronorm: personal relationships in the twenty-first century', in L. McKie, S. Cunningham-Burley and J. McKendrick (eds) *Families in Society: Boundaries and Relationships*, Bristol: Policy Press.

Roseneil, S. and Budgeon, S. (2004) 'Cultures of intimacy and care beyond "the family": personal life and social change in the early twenty-first century', *Current Sociology*, 52 (2), 135–160.

Rowbotham, S. (1972) *Women, Resistance and Revolution*, Harmondsworth: Penguin.

Ryback, D. (1997) *Putting Emotional Intelligence to Work: Successful Leadership is More than IQ*, Woburn, MA: Butterworth-Heinemann.

Sassen, S. (1998) *Globalization and its Discontents*, New York: New Press.

Sax, L. (2002) 'How common is intersex? A response to Anne Fausto-Sterling', *Journal of Sex Research*, 39 (3), 174–178.

Schiebinger, L. (1989) *The Mind Has No Sex? Women in the Origins of Modern Science*, Cambridge, MA: Harvard University Press.

Schmidt, J. (2003) 'Paradise lost? Social change and fa'afafine in Samoa', *Current Sociology*, 51 (3/4), 417–432.

Scottish Women's Aid (2007) 'What is domestic abuse? Women's Aid statistics', available at http://www.scottishwomensaid.co.uk/index.html (accessed 4 April 2007).

Segal, L. (1990) *Slow Motion: Changing Masculinities, Changing Men*, London: Virago Press.

Seidman, S. (1994) 'The new social movements and the making of new social knowledges', in S. Seidman, *Contested Knowledge: Social Theory in the Postmodern Era*, Oxford: Blackwell.

Senturia, K.D. (1997) 'A woman's work is never done: women's work and pregnancy outcome in Albania', *Medical Anthropology Quarterly*, 11 (3), 375–395.

Skeggs, B. (1997) *Formations of Class and Gender: Becoming Respectable*, London: Sage.

Slocum, S. (1975) 'Woman the gatherer: male bias in anthropology', in R.R. Reiter (ed.) *Toward and Anthropology of Women*, New York and London: Monthly Review Press, 36–50.

Smith, D. (1987) *The Everyday World as Problematic: A Feminist Sociology*. Boston, MA: Northeastern University Press.

Spender, D. (1982) *Invisible Women*, London: Writers and Readers' Publishing Co-operative.

Stanley, A. (1995) *Mothers and Daughters of Invention: Notes From a Revised History of Technology*, New Brunswick, NJ: Rutgers University Press.

Stanley, L. and Morley, A. (1988) *The Life and Death of Emily Wilding Davison*, London: The Women's Press.

Stanley, L. and Wise, S. (1983) 'Socialization and gender role: a sort of critique', in L. Stanley and S. Wise, *Breaking Out: Feminist Consciousness and Feminist Research*, London: Routledge.

Storr, M. (2002) 'Classy lingerie,' *Feminist Review*, 71 (1), 18–36.

Sullivan, O. (2006) *Changing Gender Relations, Changing Families: Tracing the Pace of Change Over Time*, Lanham, MD: Rowman & Littlefield.

Swaab, D.F., Gooren, L.J.G. and Hofman, M.A. (1995) 'Brain research, gender and sexual orientation', *Journal of Homosexuality*, 28 (3/4), 283–301.

Sydie, R.A. (1987) *Natural Women/Cultured Men: A Feminist Perspective on Sociological Theory*, Milton Keynes: Open University Press.

Thompson, J.B. (1995) *The Media and Modernity: A Social Theory of the Media*, Cambridge: Polity.

Thompson, T. (ed.) (1987) *Dear Girl: The Diaries and Letters of Two Working Women (1897–1917)*, London: The Women's Press.

Thorne, B. (1993) *Gender Play: Girls and Boys in School*, New Brunswick, NJ: Rutgers University Press.

Turner, B. (1984) *The Body in Society*, Oxford: Basil Blackwell.

UNICEF (2006) *State of the World's Children: Excluded and Invisible*, New York: UNICEF, available at http://www.unicef.org/sowc06/index.php.

Unifem: United Nations Development Fund for Women (2007) 'Facts and figures on violence against women', available at http://www.unifem.org/gender-_issues/violence_against_women (accessed December 2007).

United Nations Statistics Division (2005) 'Statistics and indicators on women and men: Table 5g – women's wages relative to men's', available at http://unstats.un.org/unsd/demographic/products/indwm/ww2005/tab5g.htm (accessed December 2007).

Urry, J. (2007) 'Contradictions and climates', seminar at Flinders University, Adelaide, 3 May. See also Lyons, G. and Urry, J. (2006) 'Foresight: the place of social science in examining the future of transport', paper presented at Evidence-Based Policies and Indicators Systems, 11–13 July, London, available at http://www.foresight.gov.uk/previous_projects/Intelligent_Infrastructure_Systems/Reports_and_Publications/Intelligent_Infrastructure_Futures/Social_Science.pdf (accessed 4 January 2008).

Vance, C.S. (ed.) (1984) *Pleasure and Danger: Exploring Female Sexuality*, London: Routledge & Kegan Paul.

Van Zoonen, L. (1995) 'Gender, representation and the media', in J. Downing, A. Mohammadi and A. Sreberny-Mohammadi (eds) *Questioning the Media*, London: Sage.

Vogel, J. (2000/1889) *Anno Domini, Or Woman's Destiny*, Auckland: Exisle
Publishing.

Walby, S. (1990) *Theorizing Patriarchy*, Oxford: Basil Blackwell.

Walby, S. (1997) *Gender Transformations*, London: Routledge.

Walker, N. (ed.) (1998) *Women's Magazines 1940–1960: Gender Roles and the Popular Press*, Boston, MA: Martin's.

Weber, M. (1968/1921) *Economy and Society*, Totowa, NJ: Bedminster Press.

Weber, M. (1981/1927) *General Economic History*, New Brunswick, NJ: Transaction
Books.

Weeks, J. (1985) *Sexuality and its Discontents: Meanings, Myths and Modern Sexualities*, London: Routledge & Kegan Paul.

Weeks, J. (2000) 'The challenge of lesbian and gay studies', in T. Sandfort, J.
Schuyf, J. Duyvendak and J. Weeks (eds) *Lesbian and Gay Studies: An Introductory, Interdisciplinary Approach*, London: Sage.

Weeks, J., Heaphy, B. and Donovan, C. (2001) *Same Sex Intimacies: Families of
Choice and Other Life Experiments*, London: Routledge.

West, C. and Zimmerman, D. (1987) 'Doing gender', *Gender and Society*, 1 (2),
125–151.

Weston, K. (1991) *Families We Choose: Lesbians, Gays, Kinship*, New York: Columbia
University Press.

Westwood, S. (2000) 'Rebranding Britain: sociology, futures and futurology', *Sociology*, 34 (1), 185–202.

Whelehan, I. (1995) *Modern Feminist Thought: From the Second-Wave to 'Post-
Feminism'*, Edinburgh: Edinburgh University Press.

Wilgoren, J. (2003) 'A new war brings new role for women', *New York Times*, 28
March.

Williams, S.J. (1998) 'Emotions, cyberspace and the "virtual" body: a critical
appraisal', in G. Bendelow and S.J. Williams (eds) *Emotions in Social Life:
Theories and Contemporary Issues*, London: Routledge, 120–134.

Willis, P. (1977) *Learning to Labour: How Working Class Kids Get Working Class Jobs*,
Farnborough, Hants: Saxon Ho.

Wind, R. (2006) 'States enacted 52 laws restricting abortion in 2005: beyond
threats to Roe v. Wade, women already face significant barriers to abortion', New York: Guttmacher Institute, 20 January, available at http://
www.agi-usa.org/media/nr/2006/01/20/index.html.

Wolf, N. (1990) *The Beauty: How Images of Beauty are Used Against Women*, New
York: Vintage.

Wollstonecraft, M. (1985/1792) *Vindication of the Rights of Woman*, Harmondsworth: Penguin.

Woolf, V. (1929) *A Room of One's Own*, New York: Harcourt & Brace.

Wouters, C. (1995) 'Etiquette books and emotion management in the 20th century: part two – the integration of the sexes', *Journal of Social History*, 29
(2), 325–340.

INDEX